MODERN FIGHTER PLANES

MILITARY AIRCRAFT

████ █ █ ████ █ █ ████ █ █ ████ █ ██

MODERN FIGHTER PLANES

George Sullivan

Facts On File
New York • Oxford

The author gratefully acknowledges permission to quote (in Chapter 13) from *Dassault-Breguet Mirage III/5*, by Salvador Mafé Huertas, published by Osprey Publishing Limited, London.

MODERN FIGHTER PLANES

Facts On File, Inc.
460 Park Avenue South
New York NY 10016
USA

Facts On File Limited
Collins Street
Oxford OX4 1XJ
United Kingdom

Library of Congress Cataloging-in-Publication Data

Sullivan, George
    Military aircraft / by George Sullivan.
        p.   cm.
    Includes index.
    Contents: v. [1] Modern fighter planes
    ISBN 0-8160-2352-2 (v. 1)
    1. Fighter planes.   I. Title
UG1242.F5S936   1991
358.4'382—dc20   91-10873

British CIP data available on request from Facts On File.

Facts On File books are available at special discounts when purchased in bulk quantities for businesses, associations, institutions or sales promotions. Please contact the Special Sales Department of our New York office at 212/683-2244 (dial 800/322-8755 except in NY, AK or HI) or in Oxford at 865/728399.

Text and jacket design by Ron Monteleone
Composition by Facts On File, Inc.
Manufactured by R. R. Donnelley & Sons, Inc.
Printed in the United States of America

10 9 8 7 6 5 4 3 2 1

This book is printed on acid-free paper.

CONTENTS

INTRODUCTION

Fast, agile, with plenty of firepower, the F-16 is the best fighter plane of the 1990s. Experts agree it can outfly any other fighter in the world.

Armed with a 20-mm cannon and Sparrow and Sidewinder air-to-air missiles, there's no plane better when it comes to intercepting and destroying enemy aircraft. The F-16 is also capable of carrying out strike missions, bombing airfields, radar stations, transportation centers—anything. The plane can carry a bomb load of almost 12,000 pounds.

That's the way it is today: Fighters can handle almost any type of mission. They're able to detect, intercept and destroy enemy aircraft in air-to-air combat; they can deliver missiles and bombs to ground targets as well.

To be able to carry out its multimission role, a fighter has to be fast. And it has to be able to reach top speed—Mach 2 and better—as quickly as possible.

Agility is just as important as speed. It comes from engine power and an aircraft's general design. In air combat, agility enables a fighter to get in a favorable position (usually high and behind the enemy). On bombing missions, agility means being able to go in low and fast.

Firepower is vital, too. Since the 1970s, developments in air-to-air missiles have revolutionized air warfare. Radar-guided and infrared missiles are among the deadly choices.

But the best technology in the world is useless without a skilled pilot. Today's fighter pilot has to know how to take his plane through a wide range of maneuvers. He also has to be able to make takeoffs and landings in bad weather, to deal with equipment breakdowns and maybe to handle an occasional collision with a seagull or other emergency.

While air combat today is very much a matter of technology—of hot planes, sophisticated weapons and supersensitive radar—tactics haven't changed very much. The key factor is still to spot the other plane first, and then to get a favorable position and fire the first shot.

When at the controls of the F-16, even with the advent of "stealth" technology, as typified by the F-117, success still comes down to pilot skill, to good eyesight and quick reflexes, and to coolness and courage.

The F-16 offers computerized flight systems, or fly-by-wire controls, as they're called. (General Dynamics)

MODERN FIGHTER PLANES

1 F-14 TOMCAT

In the troubled Middle East during the 1980s when the United States found the need to use force, it frequently called upon Navy aviation. And the plane the Navy usually singled out to meet the challenge was its "Top Gun," the Grumman F-14 Tomcat.

Take what happened early in 1989—a shootout that resulted in the downing of two Libyan MiG-23s by American pilots flying Navy F-14s from the carrier USS *John F. Kennedy*.

The deadly dogfight came as President Ronald Reagan was applying pressure on Col. Muammer el-Qaddafi, Libya's head of state, in an effort to prevent the North African nation from producing gases that could be used in chemical warfare. The United States had declared that a huge chemical plant at Rabta, about 50 miles southwest of the Libyan capital of Tripoli, was intended to produce mustard gas and other deadly chemical weapons. The Defense Department had even suggested that Tomahawk cruise missiles launched by surface ships or submarines might be used to destroy the plant.

Against this tension-filled background, two F-14s, flying at 14,000 feet, picked up a pair of Libyan MiG-23s on their radar screens. The "bogeys," as U.S. airmen call hostile planes, were about 70 miles away at 10,000 feet, and heading directly for the American planes and the *Kennedy*, which was steaming off the Libyan coast in international waters.

The F-14s changed course to turn away from the approaching aircraft, a signal that the American pilots were not looking for a fight. To the surprise of the U.S. pilots and their RIOs (radar-intercept officers), the Libyans veered abruptly—"jinked" is the word pilots use—to get back on a nose-to-nose course with the Americans. The distance between the two pairs of fighter planes, traveling at about 1,000 mph, was closing fast.

1

F-14 FACT SHEET

Manufacturer: Grumman Corporation

Type: Multimission carrier-based fighter and attack aircraft

Engines: Two General Electric F110-400 afterburning turbofans, each delivering 27,600 lb. of thrust

Crew: Pilot plus radar intercept officer

Length: 62½ ft.

Height: 16 ft.

Wingspan: 38 ft., 2 in. (swept); 64 ft., 1½ in. (spread)

Loaded Weight: 74,359 lb.

Maximum Speed: Mach 2.3+

First Flight: December 21, 1970

The F-14 can be fitted with any combination of Sidewinder, Sparrow or Phoenix missiles. Armament also includes a 20-mm multibarrel cannon.
(Grumman Corporation)

The Navy fighters sought to evade the Libyans a second time, diving to 3,000 feet. This gave the Americans a tactical advantage, for their radar now looked skyward, giving them a clear view of the approaching aircraft. The radar in the Libyan planes, scanning downward, had to contend with a jumble of signals produced by the ocean.

Another American advantage was the two-seat Tomcat. The lead plane's RIO, in the seat behind the Tomcat's pilot, coolly armed the F-14's short-range Sidewinder missiles and longer-range Sparrow rockets. In the MiG-23s, the Libyan pilots not only had to fly their planes but also watch their radar screens and get their weapons ready for firing.

The U.S. pilots made three more attempts to evade the pursuing Libyan planes. Each time, the crewmen in a nearby Navy E-2C radar plane that was monitoring the encounter heard the Libyan ground commander order the MiG pilots to jink into a head-to-head course with the F-14s.

The trailing Tomcat locked its radar on one of the MiG-23s. In the past, when Libyan pilots had reported any such radar contact to their ground controllers, they had always been ordered to break off contact and head home. This time there was no such order.

The lead Tomcat pilot then told the other airmen, "Bogeys have jinked back on me for a fifth time. They're on my nose now, inside of 20 miles."

The pilot did what he had to do. "Master arm on," he said, taking the final step before firing a Sparrow. As the planes drew even closer, he declared, "Fox 1. Fox 1." He had triggered a Sidewinder, called Fox 1. He fired one of the missiles, then another. Both missed.

Instead of fleeing, the MiG-23s continued to close in on the Tomcats. When they got within six miles, the F-14 pilots split their formation in a tried and proven maneuver. As the two MiG-23s followed the trailing plane, the lead Tomcat circled to get on the tails of the Libyan jets.

The F-14 that had been trailing fired a Sparrow, which smashed into one of the Libyan planes. "Good kill! Good kill!" shouted one of the airmen.

The other Tomcat pursued the remaining MiG-23. When it was about 1.5 miles from the plane, the F-14's RIO squeezed the trigger, and a Sidewinder headed straight for the target. "Good kill!" a crew member cried out. "Let's get out of here." The pilots of the Libyan planes parachuted into the sea.

That was not the first time that F-14s had shot down Libyan jets. In August 1981, two Navy Tomcats used Sidewinder missiles to down two Libyan Su-22s about 60 miles from the Libyan coast, after being fired

*An air-to-air view of three
F-14 Tomcats as seen from
the front seat of a fourth.*
(U.S. Navy)

on by the Libyan planes. The brief battle took place during the final
hours of a two-day United States Navy exercise in the southern Mediterranean Sea and the northern part of the Gulf of Sidra.

The story of the F-14 begins in the late 1960s, when the Navy was
beginning to seek a replacement for its fleet of aging F-4 Phantoms. At
first, the Navy thought the F-111B might meet the requirements. The
F-111B was the Navy's version of the F-111A, an Air Force fighter. But
the F-111B flunked its tests as a carrier-based plane.

The Navy then announced a design contest among manufacturers for
a new plane. The two finalists were McDonnell Douglas and the Grumman Corporation.

Grumman could point to an outstanding record in producing carrier
fighters for the Navy. Its aircraft included the rugged F6F Hellcat,
perhaps the finest carrier-based plane of World War II; the sleek and
deadly F7F Tiger Cat, a powerful fighter-bomber; and the company's
first jet fighter, the F9F Panther, which had performed impressively in
combat during the Korean War of 1950–53.

In its design competition with McDonnell Douglas in 1968, Grumman proposed a two-seat, twin-engined aircraft. Early in 1969, the Navy announced Grumman had submitted the winning entry. The new plane was designated F-14 and later named the Tomcat.

The Navy was in a hurry to get the new plane into production. So instead of designing a brand-new engine, an engine much the same as the one used in the F-111—a Pratt and Whitney TF30—was chosen for the F-14. These engines caused problems.

On December 21, 1970, at Grumman's airfield in Bethpage, Long Island, the F-14 made its first flight. Grumman began delivery to the Navy of training models of the new plane late in 1972.

The Tomcat went into operation in September 1974, aboard the USS *Enterprise*, which was assigned to the western Pacific. The first Atlantic Fleet units of the Tomcat were put to sea in June 1975 aboard the USS *John F. Kennedy*, which was bound for service in the Mediterranean. In time, the F-14 replaced the F-14 Phantom and other older fighters as the Navy's number one interceptor.

Other military aircraft have been equipped with the variable swept wings of the Tomcat. But the F-14 was the first plane to be produced in which the wing shape is controlled automatically by a computer, acting in response to the Mach number and the angle at which the wing is positioned.

For supersonic flight, the wings are swept back against the fuselage. In that position they span a distance of 38 feet, 2 inches.

When landing or taking off, the wings spread out to 64 feet, 1½ inches. This feature enables the Tomcat to land in less than 2,000 feet and take off in less than 1,000 feet. (On takeoffs, it is assisted by a catapult, of course.)

While the F-14's wings performed in expected fashion, its engines did not. They were poorly suited for the plane. There were repeated fan-blade failures, and other shortcomings having to do with reliability and durability.

The Tomcat struggled along for years, until 1981, when the present engine, a General Electric F110-400 afterburning turbofan, was introduced. This greatly improved the F-14's performance. Beginning in 1982, full-scale development of the F110 engine was begun. The F-14D is equipped with the newer engine, and many F-14As have been scheduled to undergo engine replacement.

"Defend the carrier." That's the primary job of the F-14 Tomcat.

The largest aircraft carriers, such as the *Carl Vinson*, *Dwight D. Eisenhower* and *Adm. Chester Nimitz*, carry 90 aircraft. Twenty-four of

those are F-14s. Another 24 are attack aircraft, that is, bombers—A-6 Intruders, A-7 Corsair IIs or F/A-18 Hornets.

The other aircraft have a variety of duties and responsibilities. There are E-2C Hawkeyes, judged to be the most capable electronic-warning aircraft yet produced. The Hawkeyes maintain patrols that extend the carrier's vision by hundreds of miles. There are EA-6B Prowlers, which are equipped with search radars and tactical radar-jamming pods. And there are aircraft to refuel the other aircraft, keeping them aloft for extended periods.

To guard against submarine attack, there are 10 S-3A Vikings, fixed-wing aircraft that are able to stay in the air for more than six hours at a time. The antisubmarine aircraft also include eight helicopters, SH-3A Sea Kings.

The F-14 has been provided with plenty of firepower to enable it to carry out its mission. In fact, after the pair of F-14s had shot down the two MiG-23s in 1989, aviation experts pointed out that the Libyan planes were outgunned from the start. "Bambi vs. Godzilla—that's what it was like," said Bill Sweetman, an editor for Jane's Information Group. "It was a complete mismatch."

"It's like comparing a handgun to a long-range rifle," said John Bochman, an analyst for the Center for Defense Information. The F-14 is "tremendously potent. It is one of the finest airplanes in the world."

The AIM-9 Sidewinder is the F-14's principal short-ranged weapon. For combat at medium range, the Tomcat relies on the AIM-7F Sparrow.

But perhaps the plane's most impressive weapon is the Hughes AIM-54A Phoenix, a truly long-range, air-to-air weapon. The Phoenix has been successful in destroying targets that are 100 miles away and more.

Weapons are selected to suit the particular job at hand. On one mission, the F-14 might carry six AIM-7F Sparrows and four AIM-9 Sidewinder missiles. On the next mission, the payload might be six AIM-54A Phoenix missiles and two AIM-9 Sidewinders.

That's not all. For really close encounters, the F-14 carries a Vulcan 20-mm cannon with 675 rounds of ammunition.

All of these weapons would count for little if the F-14 didn't have an effective system for controlling and firing the missile mix. In this regard, the F-14 is ahead of the pack. It uses the remarkable Hughes AWG-9 control system, which has the ability to detect targets at ranges greater than 115 miles.

Transplanted to the Tomcat from the F-111 late in 1968, the AWG-9 can track as many as 24 potential targets and, at the same time, attack six of them. It can deal with aircraft at both high and low levels. One expert calls the AWG-9 "perhaps the most outstanding feature of the entire Tomcat package."

The Tomcat's claws will be sharpened by the use of new and more effective missiles as soon as they become available. For instance, a new model of the Phoenix AIM-54 is being readied for the 1990s. It offers greater range among its other features. Newer versions of the Sparrow and Sidewinder missiles will provide increased accuracy.

In the future, the Tomcat is one of the aircraft scheduled to carry the AIM-120A radar-guided missile, widely known as AMRAAM (advanced medium-range air-to-air missile). It has greater speed, range and firepower than the Sparrow, the F-14's long-time medium-range standby.

Moreover, the AMRAAM is a "launch and leave" or "fire and forget" weapon. The pilot launches the missile in the direction of the enemy plane from a safe distance, say 40 to 50 miles, and then speeds out of

An F-14 sets down on the flight deck of the carrier America. *Note cross-deck arresting cables.*
(George Sullivan)

killing range. When the AIM-120A gets close to the enemy plane, its own radar takes over, and the missile rides those reflected beams into killing range of the enemy plane, where it explodes. By that time, the plane that fired the missile is a long distance away.

In addition to its responsibilities on interception missions, the Tomcat has also become the Navy's foremost reconnaissance aircraft. Approximately 50 Tomcats have been converted to this use through the installation of sophisticated camera equipment and infrared scanners.

Despite its role as the Navy's foremost interceptor, the Tomcat was never very successful in the overseas market. Recent customers have preferred the F-15 Eagle to the F-14.

There was one large sale, however. In 1974 and 1975, the Shah of Iran bought 80 Tomcats. The Iranians intended to use the planes against Soviet MiG-25s, which were flying over Iranian territory quite regularly. To go with the planes, the Shah also purchased 424 AIM-54A Phoenix missiles.

In 1979, the Shah was overthrown and a new government took over. The following year, open warfare broke out between Iran and Iraq. It was a long and bloody conflict. The brunt of the war in the air was borne by Iranian F-4 Phantoms and Northrop F-5 Tiger IIs. The few F-14s the Iranians were able to get off the ground were sent on reconnaissance missions, making use of their splendid radar to detect and track Iraqi

As an F-14 pilot in Top Gun, *Tom Cruise outflew and outgunned enemy MiGs.* (Showtime)

aircraft. Iraqi pilots claimed to have shot down one Tomcat during the last months of the fighting in 1988.

In 1986, F-14s played a starring role in *Top Gun*, a major Hollywood film. *Top Gun* told the story of an F-14 pilot, a lieutenant, named Pete Mitchell, nicknamed Maverick, played by Tom Cruise. First seen on an aircraft carrier patrolling the Indian Ocean, Maverick is a brash and swaggering loudmouth. Yet he manages to gain the admiration of his superiors by his coolness during a nonshooting encounter with some MiG-28s (representing some unfriendly nation that is never identified).

As a result, Maverick wins an appointment to the Navy's Advanced Fighter Weapons School at the Miramar Naval Air Station near San Diego. There he gains a beautiful female friend but loses his best male friend on a fatal aerial accident. This brings about a change in his character, making him a better person and a better pilot when he returns to the Indian Ocean.

Top Gun ends with a spectacular climax in which Maverick, in his F-14, takes on the MiG-28s.

Newsweek Magazine called *Top Gun* "a young man's macho fantasy about jet-fighter pilots, a beautiful blond flying instructor, and MiGs zapped at high altitudes." As such, it probably did more to boost the popularity of F-14s and naval aviation than anything up until then that ever happened in real life over the Mediterranean Sea or Persian Gulf.

2   F-4 PHANTOM II

Designed in the mid-1950s for the U.S. Navy, first flown by the Air Force in 1963, and produced by the thousands not only for the Navy and Air Force but for the Marine Corps as well, the versatile and durable twin-engine Phantom II ranked as the most important fighter in the Western world during the 1960s and 1970s. It is quite possibly the most famous aircraft ever to serve with the Navy.

Despite its long history, the F-4 is not yet ready for enshrinement by the National Air and Space Museum. During the war in the Persian Gulf, F-4G Wild Weasels, loaded with electronic jamming devices and HARM missiles, knocked out Iraqi ground radar and antiaircraft sites.

F-4 FACT SHEET

Manufacturer: McDonnell Aircraft Company

Type: Carrier- or land-based multimission fighter

Engines: Two General Electric J79-15 turbojets, each delivering 17,000 lb. of thrust

Crew: Pilot plus radar intercept officer (Navy) or weapons system operator (Air Force)

Length: 58 ft., 3 in.

Height: 16 ft., 3 in.

Wingspan: 38 ft., 5 in.

Loaded Weight: 60,630 lb.

Maximum Speed: Mach 2+

First Flight: May 27, 1963

In a 20-year period, Mc-Donnell Douglas built and delivered 5,197 F-4 Phantoms. (McDonnell Douglas Corporation)

Hundreds of F-4s are still on active service in the United States and with foreign air forces. By the year 2008, the 50th anniversary of the aircraft, an estimated 1,000 F-4s will still be flying, according to the McDonnell Aircraft Company, the plane's manufacturer.

The F-4 is the only fighter to have served at the same time with the Air Force, Navy and Marine Corps. It is the only aircraft to have been flown simultaneously by the air demonstration teams of the Air Force and Navy, the Thunderbirds and the Blue Angels.

The plane serves with the air forces of 11 nations besides the United States. These include Australia, Egypt, Germany, Great Britain, Greece, Iran, Israel, Japan, South Korea, Spain and Turkey.

The F-4 was used extensively in Vietnam, and it is for its heroics there that it is likely to be remembered. When the twin-engine, two-seat Phantom showed up in Vietnam in 1965, the plane was supposed to revolutionize aerial combat. The plane boasted sophisticated radar and deadly air-to-air missiles. Soviet-built MiG-17s and MiG-21s that managed to evade the medium-range Sparrow, guided to its target by the plane's radar, could be eliminated with the short-range Sidewinder, a vicious little heat-seeker that could literally fly up the enemy's white-hot tail pipe. Guns were eliminated on most Phantoms. Who needed guns? This was the age of push-button combat.

But it didn't work out like that. The first couple of years in Vietnam were a disaster for the F-4. The Sparrows seldom worked. Instead of tracking enemy planes, they sometimes tracked the sun. Or other American aircraft. Two American planes were hit by Sparrows.

When firing a Sparrow, the idea was for the pilot to point his aircraft at the target and keep pointing it for a painfully long period of time, in order to provide the beam the missile was supposed to home in on. This meant that even though the enemy plane might be only a small blip on the pilot's radar screen at the time the missile was fired, by the time the missile reached its target, the enemy plane and the F-4 were practically nose to nose. If the missile missed, a dogfight was often the result.

But the gunless F-4s weren't meant for dogfighting. The bad guys who flew the tight-turning, hard-to-spot MiG-17s and MiG-21s had 23-mm cannons in addition to their missiles, rockets and bombs. Their pilots, after a slow start, flew with skill and agressiveness. In the first half of 1967, 18 Air Force fighters were lost to MiGs. Only five enemy planes were brought down.

The experts finally realized they had been wrong. By June 1967, the F-4s were being fitted with the Vulcan 20-mm "Gatling"-style cannon. From its cluster of six revolving barrels, it fired 640 (later 1,200) rounds per minute.

In 1968, President Lyndon Johnson revised American policy in Vietnam. He cut back on the bombing and called for peace negotiations. Peace talks opened in Paris in May 1968.

The peace talks failed to produce an agreement. In March 1972, when North Vietnam began a major invasion of South Vietnam, President Nixon responded by renewing the bombing of North Vietnam. During the four-year interruption in aerial warfare, many F-4 pilots had gone through intense air-combat training. A-4 Skyhawks were used to simu-

F-4 Phantom IIs from the aircraft carrier Coral Sea *drop their bombs on North Vietnam.* (U.S. Navy)

late the MiG-17 and the way in which it performed. Northrop's F-5 played the role of MiG-21.

When F-4s tangled with MiGs for real, it was a different story. Newly developed aerial tactics enabled F-4s to outduel the MiGs in one encounter after another. There were still problems with the Sparrows. But Sidewinders had become more reliable. F-4s accounted for 107 MiG kills during the war.

While the Navy used the F-4 as an all-weather fighter, to the Marine Corps it was a fighter-bomber and interceptor. And Air Force Phantoms, flying both day and night missions, pounded North Vietnamese and Viet Cong troop positions.

Some F-4s were equipped with sophisticated attack and detection equipment to enable the planes to fly what were called "wild weasel" missions. In these, the goal was to race in, root out, and destroy enemy air-defense systems.

Aerial reconnaissance was another mission performed by the F-4. The enemy almost always moved at night, filtering through the narrow valleys over roads and trails that were protected by a canopy of jungle growth. To find the hidden foe through the curtain of darkness and thick greenery, U.S. forces installed aerial cameras and various sensors on standard reconnaissance planes, or aircraft that had been modified for spying missions. The F-4 was one of these. In time, in fact, the RF-4C, as it was designated, became the standard Air Force reconnaissance plane in Vietnam.

Infrared detectors, with which the RD-4C was equipped, were capable of locating heat sources, such as cooking fires in hidden campsites. Infrared film recorded heat variations, such as the exhausts of trucks being driven through the night. Perhaps the most unusual device of all was a "people sniffer"—a sensor that reacted to the scent given off by the human body.

One failing of the RF-4C was that it needed illumination to take photos at night. Photo-flash cartridges, which were ejected from the aircraft fuselage, provided the necessary light, but they also lit up the sky for enemy gunners.

By the time the war ended in 1975, a total of 363 F-4s had been destroyed. Most were brought down by enemy fire.

When first planned in 1954, the aircraft that was to become the F-4 was seen as a single-seat attack bomber and ground-support plane. Designated the AH-1, two examples were ordered.

Within a year, however, the plane's mission changed. The Navy now wanted a far-ranging, high-altitude interceptor—an aircraft that could be equipped with air-to-air missiles instead of a cannon. Advanced radar was another Navy request.

The weaponry and radar the Navy wanted were so sophisticated that the pilot alone could not monitor and control them while flying the plane in hostile skies. Technology had not yet advanced to a point where a computer could control these systems, as is the case with fighters today. The solution of the 1950s was to include a second crew member.

Twenty-three two-seat aircraft were ordered for testing. The plane was named the Phantom II. The "II" was added so that the aircraft would not be confused with McDonnell's F-H1 Phantom, the first jet fighter designed for carrier operations. A few of the original Phantoms were still flying.

In the newly designed plane, the pilot occupied the front cockpit. The RIO—radar intercept officer—was stationed in the rear cockpit.

Later, when the F-4 saw duty in the skies over Vietnam, there was often friendly rivalry between the two men. Traditionally independent

Guided by the Landing Safety Officer (LSO), an F-4 Phantom, its tailhook down and trailing exhaust smoke, eases in for a landing on the carrier Nimitz.
(George Sullivan)

pilots sometimes resented sharing their planes with the "guy in the back seat." They said they were "carrying around excess baggage." RIOs referred to the pilots as their "chauffeurs."

No doubt most crew members would have agreed with Bob Lewis, an executive of McDonnell Aircraft, who had flown a reconnaissance Phantom in Vietnam. Said Lewis: "I'd flown a lot of single-seat fighters, and I never once resented the other guy in the airplane. He was an essential part of the team. Besides, it was nice to have another guy to talk to when it was dark and stormy and people were shooting at you."

With the change in its combat role, the plane's designation was changed to F-4H; and later it was changed again to, simply, F-4. The first prototypes became F-4As.

Flight testing of the F-4A showed the need to make a slight increase—a mere three degrees—in the upward tilt of the plane's wings. But such a change, engineers pointed out, would require that the wing and also the landing gear retraction system be completely redesigned. Rather than make these major alterations, designers determined that tilting the outer wing panels upward 12 degrees would achieve the same results. At the same time this change was made, the aircraft's vertical tail was enlarged and the horizontal stabilizers were angled downward. These helped to give the F-4 its distinctive appearance.

During the time it was being tested, the Phantom set several speed, altitude, and time-to-climb records. On November 22, 1961, for example, the aircraft advanced the world's speed record to 1,665.89 mph. To show how high it could climb, an early Phantom II zoomed to a record altitude of 98,557 feet—almost 19 miles.

While the F-4 could tear through the sky at speeds in excess of Mach 2, it could also be flown efficiently at slow speeds. Its slowest level-flight speed was about 125 miles an hour. This characteristic is what enabled the F-4 to make safe carrier-deck landings.

A Naval Air Reserve F-4 Phantom II lands on the flight deck of the carrier America. (U.S. Navy)

It soon became apparent that the Navy's Phantoms were outperforming Air Force planes whose missions were similar to that of the F-4. As a result, the Air Force began testing the F-4 in competition with the Convair F-106, its top-of-the-line fighter at the time. The F-4 got higher marks than the F-106 in terms of the distance it could cover, size of the load it could carry, effectiveness of its radar and ease with which it could be maintained.

Little wonder that the Air Force promptly began ordering the plane, calling it the F-4C. The Air Force kept the folding wings of the Navy version of the plane, but ordered dual controls for the rear cockpit. Other changes ordered by the Air Force included bigger wheels and tires, which were needed for landings and takeoffs on asphalt runways. A total of 584 F-4Cs were purchased by the Air Force between November 1963 and February 1967.

The Marine Corps began flying the plane, too. The Marines use their air arm to support their ground forces. They want an aircraft that can remain in the battle zone for an extended period of time, rather than a hit-and-run plane. The F-4 met this qualification.

Almost from the beginning, the F-4 was hailed for its versatility. Its weapons load, carried on mountings under the wing and fuselage, can be varied to suit a variety of different missions.

As an air-to-air interceptor, the F-4 carries, besides its six-barrel 20-mm cannon, four Sidewinder and four Sparrow air-to-air missiles.

For ground attack missions, the missiles are replaced with 12 Snakeeye 500-pound bombs. For air support of ground forces, the F-4 carries six AGM-65 Maverick air-to-surface missiles. The Maverick is a launch-and-leave missile—that is, once it has been launched, the pilot can dart out of the target area.

For anti-radar attack, the F-4 is fitted out with the Wild Weasel unit. This enables the pilot to race in, detect and destroy an enemy defense system. Besides two Sidewinder and two Sparrow missiles, the F-4 carries two HARM missiles. (HARM: high-speed anti-radiation missile.) HARM missiles are replacing Shrikes, not only in the case of the F-4, but with use by other Air Force and Navy aircraft as well.

The second version of the Phantom to serve the Air Force, the F-4D, featured improvements in the plane's weapons systems, including a boost in the accuracy of the air-to-ground missiles.

The F-4E was the first Phantom to carry a built-in cannon. It was manufactured in greater numbers than any other version of the plane.

The F-4J was the second and last version of the aircraft to be produced in quantity for the Navy and Marine Corps. It had a more powerful engine—a J79-GE-10 engine delivering 17,900 pounds of thrust—and an improved radar that enabled the crew to detect aircraft flying at low altitude. A total of 522 F-4Js were built.

In 1969, the U.S. Air Force's famous aerial acrobatic team, the Thunderbirds, known officially as the U.S.A.F. Air Demonstration Squadron, switched from the F-100C Super Sabre to the F-4. The Thunderbirds had been flying Super Sabres for 13 years.

The same year, the Navy's Blue Angels, a similar team, also changed over to the F-4. It marked the first time in their history that both the Thunderbirds and the "Blues" had flown the same type of aircraft.

The Blue Angels acquired the Navy's F-4J version, while the Thunderbirds ordered the Air Force's F-4E. In both models, color-smoke-generating equipment was installed and an extra radio system added. The radio equipment was needed to better enable team members to communicate with civil air-traffic controllers. The Blue Angels' planes were repainted in their distinctive deep blue, while the Thunderbirds' aircraft were decked out in the team's familiar red, white and blue markings.

The F-4s provided the crews with added power and, at the same time, gave pilots the stability they needed when they encountered turbulent conditions at low levels during the summer show season.

In 1973, the Thunderbirds performed before more than 12 million spectators in the United States and Latin America, a record number for one year. The team's final show that season, given on November 10 in New Orleans, was also the final Thunderbird performance of the F-4.

That same year, Arab oil-producing nations had put a ban on petroleum exports to the United States. A fuel crisis gripped the nation. American motorists often had to wait in long lines to buy gasoline. The Air Force ordered the Thunderbirds to switch from the fuel-gulping F-4 to Northrup's T-38 Talon, which was much more energy-efficient. Today, the Thunderbirds fly the F-16 Fighting Falcon.

By the beginning of the 1990s, Air Force F-4s had been replaced by F-15s and F-16s in all active units, but many hundreds of Phantoms were still operational in reserve units. It was the same with the Navy. On the Navy's carrier decks, the F-4 had been replaced by F/A-18 Hornets, but large numbers remained active in both air-defense and ground-attack assignments with the Air National Guard and Air Force Reserve. As for the Marine Corps, its air wing continued to operate squadrons of F-4s not only in reserve units but at the Marine Corps Air Station, Kaneohe Bay, Hawaii, where they were scheduled to remain until 1993.

3   MiG-23 (FLOGGER)

The MiG-23, with its variable swept wing, is often compared to the F-4 Phantom. The Soviet plane, however, is faster and more agile than the F-4.
(National Air and Space Museum)

Built in greater quantity during the 1970s and 1980s than any other combat aircraft in the world, the MiG-23 is not simply one type of plane but an entire "family" of interceptors, fighter-bombers and trainers. All versions, however, have virtually the same airframe.

The MiG-23's variable swept wing, similar to that of the Navy's F-14 Tomcat, is one of the chief reasons the plane has proven so versatile. In

MiG-23 FACT SHEET

Designer: Mikoyan/Gurevich OKB

Type: Multimission fighter and attack aircraft

Engine: One Tumansky R-29 afterburning turbojet, delivering 27,560 lb. of thrust

Crew: Pilot only

Length: 55 ft., 1½ in.

Height: 14 ft., 4 in.

Wingspan: 26 ft., 10 in.

Loaded Weight: 44,300 lb.

Maximum Speed: Mach 2.35

First Flight: 1966

---

its fully forward position, the wing provides tremendous lift, enabling the aircraft to carry heavy loads of fuel and weapons. Short takeoff and landing runs are another advantage.

When the wings are swept back and drag is reduced, the MiG-23 is ready for air-to-air interception missions or hit-and-run attacks on enemy ground targets.

The MiG-23 is often compared to the F-4 Phantom. While not as heavily armed as the F-4, the MiG-23 is more maneuverable and slightly faster than the American-built plane. The MiG-23 has a combat radius of 600 miles and a combat ceiling of 59,000 feet.

For years, the MiG-23 served as the standard fighter of the Warsaw Pact countries. These were Communist nations of Europe that were bound together in a military command under the control of the Soviet Union. They signed the Warsaw Pact in the city of Warsaw, Poland, in 1955, claiming the pact came about in response to the creation of the North Atlantic Treaty Organization (NATO), an alliance formed by the United States and its European allies in 1949. Warsaw Pact nations that ordered the MiG-23 included Bulgaria, Czechoslovakia, East Germany, Hungary, Poland and Rumania. The MiG-23 was also flown by Algeria, Cuba, Egypt, Ethiopia, India, Iraq, Libya, North Korea, Sudan, Syria and Vietnam.

Syria often used its Soviet-built planes to play cat-and-mouse games over Lebanon with Israeli aircraft. Both the 1967 and 1973 Arab-Israeli wars were preceded by Syrian-Israeli dogfights.

There were skirmishes during the 1980s, too. Israeli fighter planes flew reconnaissance missions over Lebanon several days a week. Besides the planes doing the photographing, the Israelis used several American-built F-15s or F-16s to provide air cover. In addition, the reconnaissance team benefited from the presence of an EC-2 Hawkeye, an aircraft with advanced radar systems. The Hawkeye was able to detect Syrian fighters as they took off from their bases.

One November day in 1985, a pair of Israeli jets were patrolling inside Lebanon and had reached the northernmost point of their mission when two Syrian MiG-23s were detected heading toward them. Soon the Syrian planes were within what the Israeli pilots considered to be their "danger range"—the range within which the Syrian planes would be able to hit the Israelis with their cannons and missiles.

The MiG-23 was once the standard fighter of the Warsaw Pact nations—Bulgaria, Czechoslovakia, East Germany, Hungary, Poland and Romania.
(U.S. Navy)

The reconnaissance planes called in their air cover. A short dogfight followed. The two Syrian MiG-23s were shot down. Said an Israeli spokesperson: "A hot situation was generated in which we had no option but to respond."

MiGs are the best known of all Soviet military aircraft. MiGs were the planes that engaged American planes in combat during the Korean and Vietnam Wars.

The term "MiG" is derived from the names of Artem I. Mikoyan and Mikhail I. Gurevich, the most noted Soviet aircraft designers. The "i" in MiG is the first letter of the Russian word for "and."

Not all Soviet aircraft are called MiGs. The term refers to only one of several of the Soviet Union's OKBs. OKB stands for Optyno-Konstruktorskoye Byuro, or Experimental Construction Bureau. The fighter planes of the Soviet Air Force, as well as its bombers, tankers, trainers and other aircraft are output of the OKBs.

Second in importance to the MiG is the OKB named for Pavel A. Sukhoi, another famous aircraft designer. Such aircraft as the Su-24 Fencer, all-weather attack and reconnaissance plane, and the Su-27 Flanker, a long-range multipurpose fighter, are products of the Sukhoi OKB.

The OKB of Andrei N. Tupolev designs and builds large multi-engined bombers. Two examples: The Tu-22 Blinder and the Tu-26 Backfire.

In their earliest days, each OKB was made up of a small design team. But today, they are huge government bureaus. The original designers are dead. Gurevich died in 1950; Mikoyan, in 1970.

Besides the two or three letters that stand for the names of the designer or designers, Soviet aircraft are also identified by a two-digit number. Odd numbers are assigned to fighters and fighter-bombers; even numbers go to large multi-engine bombers and transport planes.

During the cold-war years of the 1970s and 1980s, the Soviets seldom volunteered any information about their aircraft. They didn't even disclose how they were to be designated. Not until they were ready to sell an airplane in foreign markets did the Soviets identify it by number. Other times such information would be revealed in treaty negotiations.

This hampered the NATO nations. To help clarify matters, NATO developed its own system of identifying Soviet aircraft. As soon as a Soviet plane was photographed for the first time, it was given a name that began with the letter of its type—"F" for fighters, "B" for bombers. That is how we happen to have Soviet fighters named Flogger, Frogfoot and Fulcrum, and such bombers as Blinder, Backfire and Bear.

The MiG design bureau began work on the MiG-23 in 1955. It was to be a very different design from earlier Soviet combat aircraft. Planes such as the MiG-17, MiG-19 and MiG-21 had one job to do, and one job only. That was to keep opposing planes from attacking Soviet ground forces. The MiG-23 was planned as a multimission aircraft.

Earlier MiGs, such as the MiG-21 (shown in illustration), MiG-19 and MiG-17, had one job to do: Keep opposing planes from attacking Soviet ground forces. (National Air and Space Museum)

Two prototypes were built. It was a relatively small plane with Mach 2 speed. Because the Soviet Union kept the project tightly cloaked in secrecy, little was ever learned of the aircraft, even after it had been flight-tested. It was probably first flown in the summer of 1966. The aircraft was first publicly demonstrated at the Domodedova air show, not far from Moscow, in 1967.

While the first models of the MiG-23 were intended primarily for intercept missions, the fact that the aircraft was equipped with a laser rangefinder and sophisticated radar indicated the Flogger was also intended to play a role as an attack aircraft. In time, it replaced the MiG-21 Fishbed as the Soviet Union's number-one combat aircraft.

In time, the many versions of the MiG-23 came to include the following:

MiG-23M, Flogger B—The first production model, a single-seat interceptor. Deliveries to the Soviet Air Force began in 1972.

MiG-23MF, Flogger B—An interceptor similar to the MiG-23M, but with a more powerful engine and upgraded radars. The first Soviet aircraft with the ability to track and engage enemy aircraft flying at an altitude below its own. Deliveries began in 1978.

MiG-23UM, Flogger C—A two-seater used as both a trainer and combat aircraft. Identical to the MiG-23M except for the second cockpit.

MiG-23B/27, Flogger D—A fighter-bomber with the upgraded engine of the MiG-23MF, Flogger B.

MiG-23MS, Flogger E—An interceptor, the export version of the MiG-23M. No infrared sensor and less powerful radars.

MiG-23BN, Flogger F—A fighter-bomber, the export version of the MiG-27, Flogger D. It has the same nose shape, armor plate and laser rangefinder of the MiG-27, but retains the engine and twin-barrel gun of the MiG-23MF.

MiG-23ML; Flogger G—An interceptor similar to the MiG-23MF, but with a smaller tail, lighter-weight radar and a newly designed sensor pod beneath the nose.

MiG-23BM; Flogger H—Similar to the MiG-23BN, Flogger F, but with radar-warning receivers on each side beneath the bottom of the fuselage.

MiG-23; Flogger K—Similar to the MiG-23ML, Flogger G, but with improvements to the wing that make for increased stability. It was also modified to carry close range air-to-air missiles.

During the 1980s, approximately 1,000 Floggers were on active duty with the Soviet strategic air defense force, and another thousand were available for tactical duty. The United States Air Force expects the MiG-23 "to serve in sizeable numbers" through the mid-1990s.

4 F-5

Small and simple with razor-thin wings, the Northrop Corporation's needle-nosed F-5 and the fighter models derived from it offered performance and capability out of proportion to their size. Although it is not being produced any more, the F-5 led a global life of color and excitement for 30 years.

Because the F-5 was cheap, light in weight and a cinch to handle, it found a ready market in every corner of the world. An alphabetical list of nations that flew—and continue to fly—the aircraft (see below) looks like an index from a world atlas.

F-5 FACT SHEET

Manufacturer: Northrop Corporation

Type: Tactical fighter

Engines: Two General Electric J85 turbojets, each delivering 4,000 lb. of thrust

Crew: Pilot plus radar intercept officer (Navy) or weapons system operator (Air Force)

Length: 58 ft., 3 in.

Height: 16 ft., 3 in.

Wingspan: 38 ft., 5 in.

Loaded Weight: 60,630 lb.

Maximum Speed: Mach 2+

First Flight: May 27, 1963

F-5s helped to defend South Vietnam until the country surrendered in 1975.
(Northrop Corporation)

The F-5 had its beginnings in the mid-1950s. The Korean War, which ended in 1953, had demonstrated America's need for a low-cost, easy-to-operate, high-performance fighter. Northrop began design work on such a plane in 1955.

For a time, the United States Navy was interested in the aircraft. In 1956, however, the Navy withdrew its support. The Air Force's enthusiasm also dimmed. The Air Force ordered only a trainer version of the plane, known as the T-38 Talon.

Northrop didn't give up on the F-5. The result was the F-5A Freedom Fighter, purchased in large numbers by the Department of Defense during the early 1960s for delivery to what were called "free world" countries. Bahrain, Brazil, Canada, Chile, Ethiopia, Greece, Honduras, Indonesia, Iran, Jordan, Kenya, South Korea, Libya, Malaysia, Mexico, Morocco, the Netherlands, Norway, the Philippines, Saudi Arabia,

A pair of F-5Es arrive at the Miramar Naval Air Station near San Diego, California, for use by the Naval Fighter Weapons School to simulate the flight characteristics of enemy fighters in air-to-air combat training of Navy pilots.
(Northrop Corporation)

Singapore, Spain, Sudan, Taiwan, Thailand, Tunisia, Turkey, Venezuela, Vietnam and Yemen—all began flying the plane.

Though the F-5 was somewhat handicapped by its inability to carry a big payload, it was more than a match for many other fighters of the day. Its afterburner enabled the plane to fly at supersonic speed, but only for bursts of a few seconds because it carried so little fuel. In pilot terminology, the F-5 had "short legs."

But the aircraft was acclaimed for its simplicity. Its instrument panel was less complicated than that of most single-engine private planes. Because it was such an uncomplicated machine, the F-5 was easy to maintain and repair.

The F-5's weaponry included two Sidewinder missiles on wingtip launchers, and two 20-mm guns in the nose. Five pylons, one under the fuselage and two under each wing, enabled the plane to carry a wide variety of bombs and missiles.

Enroute to Jordan, an F-5 is loaded into a C-5 Galaxy transport. (U.S. Air Force)

From October 1965 to March 1966, a squadron of 12 F-5A Freedom Fighters flew hundreds of combat missions in Vietnam. They bombed enemy troop positions and supply dumps, escorted bombers and provided armed reconnaissance.

During 1966, the United States Air Force trained South Vietnamese pilots to fly the F-5A at Williams Air Force Base, not far from Mesa, Arizona. The South Vietnamese pilots returned to South Vietnam to fly training missions with the plane. By January 1967, they were ready to fly combat missions. That month, in a formal ceremony at Bien Hoa, a tactical airfield in South Vietnam, the Air Force officially turned the planes over to the South Vietnamese 522nd Fighter Squadron.

As the fighting continued, the Air Force continued to supply F-5As and the improved F-5E to the South Vietnamese. The aircraft helped to defend South Vietnam until the nation's surrender in 1975.

After the war, the F-5E, now nicknamed the Tiger II, found another role to play. It became an "aggressor" aircraft in mock aerial-combat duels. At the Air Combat Maneuvers Range in Yuma, Arizona, the F-5 was always the "enemy" fighter. It was painted in the colors of the "enemy" nation. Its pilot was assigned to duplicate the flight characteristics of the "enemy" aircraft. F-15 and F-16 pilots who opposed the highly maneuverable F-5E described it as "a hard nut to crack." Often the F-5E emerged the "winner" in such duels.

The Navy purchased its first F-5s (F-5Fs) in 1974. The planes were assigned to Top Gun, the nickname for the Navy's Fighter Weapons School at the Miramar Naval Air Station near San Diego, California. Air crewmen trained at Top Gun experience the most intense combat flying there is, outside of actual combat. At Top Gun, the F-5F simulated the Soviet Union's MiG-21, which it happened to resemble in both size and flight characteristics. The "good guys" at Top Gun flew F-14s or F/A-18s.

The movie *Top Gun*, which was released in 1986, featured F-5Es in a number of scenes. But few of the millions who saw the film realized it. That's because the F-5Fs were done up in black latex paint and cast as the dreaded Commie "MiG-28s." They were flown in the film by Top Gun pilots.

This two-seat version of the F-5 was designated the F-5B. (Northrop International)

Production of the F-5 continued up until the late 1980s. By that time, more than 3,600 F-5s had been produced. The plane was in use in air forces all over the world, and it continued in its "enemy" role at U.S. Navy and Air Force training schools.

Northrop's successor to the F-5 was the F-20 Tigershark, which incorporated many features of the F-5. Like the F-5, a high-performance aircraft, the F-20 could climb faster, accelerate more rapidly, and make tighter turns than any aircraft it was ever likely to encounter.

Pilots who flew the F-20 Tigershark, which was extensively flight-tested during the mid-1980s, said it was as capable in a dogfight as the F-16. And the F-20 cost less.

But neither the United States Department of Defense nor any foreign governments ever showed very much interest in the F-20. In 1989, after having spend about $1 billion in development costs, Northrop discontinued the plane.

Some observers said the F-5 was one reason why the F-20 was unsuccessful. Those who owned F-5s were very satisfied with what they had. Why bother to change, they figured.

5　AV-8B HARRIER II

A Marine Corps ground unit is pinned down under heavy fire. The unit commander calls for air support. From a nearby clearing, an AV-8B Harrier II hurries into the air and streaks for the battlefield. Within minutes, the Harrier is on the scene, pounding the enemy from treetop level with its bombs and Maverick air-to-surface missiles.

The AV-8B Harrier II is like no other plane operated by the American armed forces. It is a short-takeoff and vertical-landing (STO/VL) aircraft. Its unique ability enables the Harrier II to land on and take off

A short takeoff and landing plane, the AV-8B Harrier is unlike any other flown by United States armed forces. (McDonnell Douglas Corporation)

AV-8B FACT SHEET

Manufacturer: McDonnell Aircraft Company

Major Subcontractor: British Aerospace

Type: Close air support and interdiction missions

Engine: Rolls-Royce Pegasus II turbofan, delivering 21,450 lb. of thrust

Crew: Pilot only

Length: 46 ft., 4 in.

Height: 11 ft., 8 in.

Wingspan: 30 ft., 4 in.

Loaded Weight: 31,000 lb.

Maximum Speed: 0.91 Mach

First Flight: November 9, 1978

from an area no bigger than a tennis court. It can be a cleared rectangle in the jungle, a narrow strip of road, a bomb-damaged runway, or the deck of an amphibious assault ship. No sprawling air base nor lumbering aircraft carrier is needed.

The same system of rotating nozzles—what's called a "vectored thrust" system—that enables the Harrier II to take off and land vertically also permits the aircraft to perform maneuvers in air-to-air combat that are impossible for any other fighter. From forward flight, the Harrier can suddenly shoot straight upward. Or it can appear to make an abrupt stop and then fly backwards. This is called "viffing" (from vectoring in forward flight, or VIFF). Not only is the Harrier an unbelievably maneuverable aircraft, but it is able to maintain its maneuverability at slow speeds.

From his raised cockpit with its bubble canopy, offering 360 degrees of visibility, the Harrier pilot operates the most modern controls available. His chief flight instrument is a video display that presents flight, navigation and weapons information directly in his line of vision. It's called HUD—head-up display. It is designed, as are other cockpit instruments, to eliminate the pilot's "head down" time. With HUD, a pilot can concentrate on flying. He never has to search the cockpit for needed information.

The Harrier II can carry a wide variety of weapons on seven ordnance mountings, one beneath the fuselage and six beneath the wing. These include laser-guided weapons, conventional or cluster bombs, air-to-ground missiles such as the Maverick, and self-defense air-to-air missiles such as the Sidewinder. A fuselage-mounted 25-mm cannon gives the pilot yet another weapon for air-to-air or air-to-ground combat.

But the Harrier's greatest asset is that it's never far from the fight, and thus always able to provide quick support for ground troops. Not only does it have the flexibility of a helicopter when it comes to takeoffs and landings, but once it arrives over its target it boasts the firepower of a strike fighter. Little wonder that the Royal Air Force and the United States Marine Corps operate hundreds of Harriers.

When the jet engine was developed toward the end of World War II, there was a great rush among the warring nations to combine the new invention with the fighter plane. Germany introduced in 1944 the Messerschmidt Me.262 Schwalbe (or swallow: a small, swift bird), a deadly fighter that scored one victory after another over the U.S. Air Force's four-engined B-17s and B-24s.

The United States answered Germany's challenge with the F-80 Shooting Star, designed and tested by the Lockheed Corporation. Test-flown in 1944, the F-80 boasted a maximum speed of 580 mph, some one hundred miles-an-hour faster than the best fighters of the time.

After the war ended in 1945, aircraft designers began to think of other uses for the powerful jet engines and the tremendous thrust they were capable of developing. Vertical takeoff was one such possibility.

There were obvious advantages to an airplane that could take off vertically like a rocket. The most obvious was that no long runway would be needed. An aircraft that could take off vertically required about the same amount of space as occupied by a living room carpet. Three or four could take off from a midcity parking lot.

The concept of vertical takeoff was of much greater interest to British than American aircraft designers. In the early 1950s, Great Britain's Rolls-Royce Corporation began to conduct vertical-takeoff experiments. Engineers mounted two Rolls-Royce turbojet engines on a squarish, tubular-steel frame, and modified the engine tailpipes so the jet exhaust was directed downward. When the engines were fired, the steel frame, perched on four spindly legs, rose into the air, looking as if it had been hauled upward by an invisible crane. The invention, nicknamed the "Flying Bedstead," could also hover like a helicopter. It created a worldwide sensation.

During the mid-1950s, the Flying Bedstead made hundreds of flights and triggered countless newspaper articles and magazine stories about Vertical Takeoff and Landing (VTOL) airliners operating from midtown terminals of the world's largest cities. No airports, or the delays associated with them, would be necessary.

The vision prompted Rolls-Royce to develop a special series of powerful but lightweight turbojet engines meant for vertical-lift aircraft. These engines eventually powered the world's first VTOL aircraft, the SC-1, a delta-winged plane with five Rolls-Royce RB.108s. Four of these engines were mounted vertically in pairs to provide lift. Once the plane was airborne, the fifth engine, mounted horizontally, drove it forward.

The SC-1 was intended to be a forerunner of a single-seat VTOL fighter, which would use a more powerful version of the RB.108 engine. It was looked upon as a scaled-down version of the much larger VTOL airliner.

Meanwhile, another British company, Hawker-Siddeley (which later was to become British Aerospace), was also at work developing a workable lift system for jet aircraft. It was called the vectored-thrust system. In this, the jet engine exhaust was directed through four rotating nozzles. For vertical takeoff or landing, the nozzles were swiveled to direct the thrust downward. For forward flight, the nozzles were rotated to the rear to give horizontal thrust. It was this system that was to be used on the Harrier.

Vectored thrust was first tried on the Hawker P.1127, which made its first successful flight in 1961. "Successful" for the P.1127 meant the aircraft took off vertically, flew forward and then landed vertically.

Development of an improved version of the P.1127, called the Kestral (a kestral is a small falcon), began in 1974. Nine Kestrals were built, and a squadron of pilots from the United States, Great Britain and West Germany began flying them.

The test flights were so promising that the Royal Air Force ordered the development of an improved version of the Kestral, with a more powerful engine and a complete weapons system. In 1967, this plane was named the Harrier (a harrier is a type of hawk that hunts over marshes and meadows).

Meanwhile, other manufacturers were becoming interested in VTOL aircraft. In France, the Marcel Dassault Corporation began adapting one of its Mirage fighters to take off vertically. A German company, Dornier, announced plans for a VTOL transport plane.

In the United States, Lockheed led the way. In 1963, Lockheed built and flew the XV-4A, a test version of a VTOL fighter. Named the Hummingbird, the XV-4A was a midwing monoplane that was powered by a pair of Pratt and Whitney turbojets. Although the plane performed with some success, it never went into large-scale production.

Other American companies that tinkered with VTOL aircraft included Ryan Aeronautical, the Boeing Company and Bell Aerosystems, a helicopter manufacturer.

The U.S. Department of Defense was also interested in the concept. Between 1950 and 1970, American military authorities sponsored the testing of many different kinds of VTOL systems. None, however, was as simple, practical or successful as the vectored-thrust principle pioneered in Great Britain.

In 1971, the U.S. Marine Corps, aware of the ability of VTOL technology to provide support for its ground forces, ordered three AV-8A Harriers for testing and evaluation. The planes quickly demon-

A Marine AV-8B practices low-level flying over the Nevada desert during training exercises at the Naval Air Station, Fallon, Nevada. (McDonnell Douglas Corporation)

strated the benefits of VTOL aircraft, but marine pilots found the plane to be limited in range and in the amount of weapons it could carry.

To help solve these problems, a project of international cooperation was launched. It involved McDonnell Douglas, an American company, and British Aerospace. Out of this joint undertaking came the AV-8B Harrier II.

One of the Harrier II's most interesting innovations had to do with the material from which the plane's wings and many other parts were made. The Harrier I's wing was made of metal. The Harrier II's wing, like the wing of the plane that the Wright Brothers flew at Kitty Hawk, is cloth—a special kind of cloth, to be sure.

Carbon fibers are woven into cloth form, and cut and shaped. The cloth pieces are then treated with epoxy resin under heat and pressure. The result is a material that resembles a steel spider web, as strong as the toughest metal but as light as aluminum.

Not only is the skin of the Harrier II's wing made of carbon fiber, the wing spars (the structural parts within the wing) are carbon-fiber composites, too. The all-composite wing of the Harrier II is 330 pounds lighter than would be a metal wing of the same size.

In addition to the wing, other composite parts on the AV-8BII include the rudder, ailerons and the forward fuselage. Besides reducing weight, composite parts, because they do not corrode, have a much longer structural life than metal parts.

Not only does Great Britain's Royal Air Force operate a fleet of Harriers, so does the Royal Navy. This plane is called the Sea Harrier. It has improved electronics and radar, plus a raised cockpit, made necessary by having to fit all that new gear into the plane.

Sea Harriers operate from amphibious assault ships, aircraft carriers, and other types of seagoing platforms. Unlike other carrier aircraft, the Harrier doesn't have to be loaded into a catapult to be launched, nor, when landing, brought to a stop with special arresting gear.

There's never any need for a carrier to change course—that is, to head into the wind—when a Harrier is taking off. The plane can even take to the air when the carrier is taking on fuel or stores at sea, or when the ship is in port and at anchor.

Great Britain's seagoing Harriers had a chance to prove themselves in combat in 1982. The Falkland Islands, a group of about 200 green, hilly and windswept islands in the South Atlantic, about 30 miles east of the Strait of Magellan, were the scene of the conflict. Both Great Britain and Argentina claimed to own the islands, which, to the Argentines, are known as the Islas Malvinas.

The islands of East Falkland and West Falkland contain most of the nation's population, estimated at 2,000. Sheep-raising is the chief occupation of the Falklands, wool the main export.

British settlers first occupied the Falklands in 1765. Eleven years later, according to Argentine historians, Great Britain yielded its claim to the islands and gave them to Spain.

During the early decades of the next century, Argentina gained its independence from Spain and then laid claim to the Falklands. Argentina sent settlers to the Falklands in 1831, but they were expelled by a British expedition in 1833. The islands were then settled by the British.

But the Argentines never gave up their claims to the Falklands. In 1982, when the Argentines became frustrated with the way negotiations were going, they sent an invasion force to attack the islands. By April 2nd that year, the Argentines had taken control.

The British were outraged. Despite efforts by the United Nations and the United States to mediate the crisis, the British sent a large task force of troops, ships and planes to the Falklands.

Marine AV-8Bs from the Marine Corps Air Station at Cherry Point, North Carolina, fly in formation over California's Sierra Nevada mountain range. (McDonnell Douglas Corporation)

Fighting began early in May. In the first clashes, British torpedoes sank the Argentine cruiser *General Belgrade*. Not long after, an Argentine missile destroyed the *Sheffield*, a British destroyer.

The British fleet included the carrier *Hermes* and *Invincible*. For aircraft, all they offered were 33 Sea King helicopters and 36 Sea Harriers. These were opposed by 223 Argentine combat planes, including 79 American-built A-4 Skyhawks—a single-seat attack aircraft.

In one air battle, the Argentines lost a dozen planes. Most of them fell victim to the Sea Harriers. They startled Argentine pilots with their ability to maneuver sideways, upward, and even backward. A Harrier would wait for an enemy aircraft to fly past and then deliver a death blow from behind with its 25-mm gun or Sidewinder missiles. It was like something out of Star Wars.

That wasn't all the Harriers did. Using the carriers as air bases, they attacked troop positions with anti-personnel bombs. They struck at airstrips and other Argentine strongholds. They flew reconnaissance missions. And they dropped thousands of leaflets urging the Argentines to surrender. Each leaflet contained a safe-conduct pass in both Spanish and English.

Eventually, British troops, who landed in great numbers on the most populated islands, surrounded Argentine forces clustered in the capital of Stanley on East Falkland Island, and forced them to surrender. By mid-June, fighting had ended and the British were back in charge. The Falklands have been quiet ever since.

Since 1989, the United States Marine Corps has been operating Harrier IIs equipped for night missions. These aircraft offer an infrared sensor that "sees" in the dark. Located in the nose of the airplane, the sensor provides the pilot with a video picture of the scene ahead on a wide-field-of-view display. Resembling a green and white picture on a TV screen, the video display helps the pilot locate and identify targets for ground attack.

Another feature in the nighttime attack system is a digital moving map, which is available to the pilot in another video display. The map is programmed on a laser disk before the flight. Not only does the map contain the navigational features of the area over which the pilot is flying, it also discloses intelligence information. Best of all, it does away with the difficult chore of trying to read from a hand-held map or chart in a dark and crowded cockpit.

Pilots flying at night wear night-vision goggles. Similar to those worn by infantry troops, they help the pilot identify and track targets outside the infrared sensor's field of view.

The standard white lighting of the cockpit instrument panel gets changed to blue-green for nighttime flying. White was found to be too bright for night vision goggles, and limited their effectiveness.

The Harrier II is also operated by the Spanish Navy, which uses the aircraft for reconnaissance as well as air-to-ground attack missions. The Spanish call the plane the Matador. The same Sea Harrier that was developed for the Royal Navy is also operated by the Indian Navy.

The Soviet Union has developed a STOL (short takeoff and landing) fighter. One such aircraft, adapted from the delta-winged MiG-21, has been exhibited at Soviet air shows. NATO has named the plane the Faithless.

A number of American airframe manufacturers are experimenting with the STOL concept. Will the vision of a STOL commercial airliner ever be realized? Nobody can say for sure. The advantage of being able to take off and land in the center of a heavily populated city is obvious to anyone who has traveled by air in recent years. Because of traffic delays and distances involved, the trip to the airport is frequently longer in time than the plane trip.

But one problem with STOL aircraft is the tremendous amount of noise they generate on takeoffs and landings. It would never be tolerated in any midtown area. If that problem could be solved, the STOL airliner would have a much greater chance of becoming a reality. In the meantime, the AV-8B Harrier II is pointing the way.

6   MiG-25 (FOXBAT)

During the late 1950s, the United States began development of an impressive new bomber, an airplane that was to have a cruising speed of 2,000 miles an hour, or more than three times the speed of sound. It was to be able to cruise at an altitude of 70,000 feet. Called the B-70 Valkyrie, this awesome plane made its first flight in 1964.

News of the new Mach 3 bomber shook military experts in the Soviet Union. They assigned the MiG design bureau to develop an interceptor that would be able to meet the challenge of the B-70.

An MiG-25 set the world speed record in 1967, hitting 1,853.61 miles per hour. (U.S. Navy)

MiG-25 FACT SHEET

Designer: Mikoyan/Gurevich OKB

Type: High-altitude interceptor

Engines: Two Tumansky R-31 afterburning turbojets, each delivering 27,120 lb. of thrust

Crew: Pilot only

Length: 73 ft., 2 in.

Height: 18 ft., 4½ in.

Wingspan: 45 ft., 9 in.

Loaded Weight: 79,800 lb.

Maximum Speed: Mach 2.8+

First Flight: 1964

When President Lyndon Johnson abruptly canceled the B-70 project in 1967, the Soviets already had their interceptor. They called it the MiG-25. To NATO, it was the Foxbat. It was the fastest combat aircraft ever put in front-line service.

The MiG-25 flew for the first time in 1964 and began showing up in American satellite reconnaissance photos and on radar tracking screens in the years that followed. Powered by two large turbojets, each capable of producing more than 25,000 pounds of thrust, the MiG-25 cruised at Mach 2.7 and was capable of speeds of Mach 3.2 and 3.3 It could climb to 36,000 feet in two and one-half minutes, and operated with ease at altitudes of 70,000 to 80,000 feet. Such performance statistics sent a chill through the United States defense establishment.

The MiG-25 caused more worried frowns in September 1967, when it set a world speed record, blazing through the sky at 1,853.61 miles an hour over a 310-mile course. (The record stood for more than a decade, until topped by an American SR-71 in July 1976. The SR-71 flew at 2,016 miles per hour.)

The MiG-25 was seen publicly and thoroughly photographed at the Domodedevo air show outside Moscow in 1968. Afterward, there were more cries of alarm. Newspapers of the day created the idea that the MiG-25 was a super aircraft, one that would pose a tremendous threat to America's air supremacy in any future conflict. Robert Seamans, Secretary of the United States Air Force, described the MiG-25 as "probably the best interceptor in production in the world today." The United States aerospace industry peddled bumperstickers and buttons that said "Stamp out Foxbats."

For years, a reconnaissance version of the MiG-25 flew at will over Israel, Iran, China, the North Sea, the Mediterranean and the Persian Gulf. No nation had the ability to shoot it down. The Israelis tried with F-4 Phantoms armed with Sparrow missiles, and failed.

The MiG-25 continued to reign supreme until the early 1970s. That's when the Navy's F-14 Tomcat, which was equipped with Phoenix missiles, arrived upon the scene. Strictly as a reconnaissance plane, the Foxbat was unchallenged until Lockheed's SR-71 became operational in the late 1960s and early 1970s.

Late in the summer of 1976, intelligence experts got a rare opportunity to examine a Foxbat firsthand. A Soviet Air Force lieutenant flew his MiG-25 across the 200-mile breadth of the Sea of Japan, landing in Japan at Hakodate on the northern Japanese island of Hokkaido. He circled the airport twice before landing, putting out his drag chute to slow down. Even so, he overshot the runway by about 800 feet.

The pilot's name was Lieut. Viktor I. Belenko. He told Japanese police who questioned him that he was fleeing the repressive Communist rule in the Soviet Union and was seeking refuge in the United States. (Intelligence sources later said, however, that there were other reasons for his flight, one of which was an unhappy marriage.)

George Bush, who in another 12 years would be elected America's president, was director of the Central Intelligence Agency at the time. Bush said the defection of Lieut. Belenko from the Soviet Union at the controls of his MiG-25 was "probably a major intelligence bonanza" for the United States and its allies.

President Gerald Ford offered Lieut. Belenko asylum in the United States, which he accepted. In his first weeks in the country, he was questioned almost continuously by United States intelligence officials.

In addition to providing information about the MiG-25, he gave his questioners some insight into what life was like for a fighter pilot in the Soviet Union. Lieut. Belenko said he was assigned to the air base at Sakharovka, about 160 miles northeast of Vladivostok, a major seaport city on Russia's eastern coast. A typical week began on Monday morning when he was told what day he would be flying. If he happened to be flying on Tuesday, he would spend the rest of Monday drafting his flight plan as well as alternative flight plans.

He would be given a cockpit checkout by his flight chief, and a safety examination. Both his squadron commander and regimental commander had to certify his fitness to fly.

On Tuesday morning, the safety instructor would first fly the airplane to check weather conditions. Belenko would then be given another test in safety procedures. Finally he received a preflight medical examination, which included questions relating to his psychological fitness. And only then would he be allowed to take the plane up.

At the time of his defection, Belenko had flown only 30 hours in the MiG-25. He explained that was because the plane was normally flown automatically by ground controllers, except for takeoffs and landings.

Belenko said that one of the drawbacks of the MiG-25 was that it was a "straight line" aircraft, with little maneuverability. It took a considerable amount of time for the plane to work up to its full speed, and all the while it was burning fuel at a tremendous rate.

When the lieutenant visited a United States aircraft carrier, he was astounded by the easygoing military procedures. He found it hard to believe that the carrier crew handled the aircraft takeoffs and launchings "without ever being given an order and without anyone shouting at them." He was also surprised by the huge portions of food "served free and at all times" to the sailors. He repeatedly asked how much each portion of food cost.

While Soviet officials fumed, Japanese and American experts began taking the MiG-25 apart and examining it piece by piece. Some things impressed them about the plane; others didn't.

Experts were surprised to find the MiG-25 had parts made of steel alloys in the wings and fuselage. At the time, titanium, a light, heat-resistant and very expensive metal was being used in the United States in the manufacture of United States supersonic aircraft.

While using steel kept the MiG-25's cost low, it added to the plane's weight. To compensate for the extra weight, stronger engines were required. These gulped down large amounts of fuel and reduced the aircraft's range.

Intelligence reports had given the MiG-25 a top speed of Mach 3. But the plane indicator stopped at Mach 2.8, and the last figure was printed in red, indicating danger.

Some aspects of the investigation focused on the MiG-25's radar, which was described as being more powerful than any other radar equipment then in use. Being more powerful meant, for one thing, that it was less vulnerable to jamming by enemy electronic devices.

But the Foxbat's radar lacked a "look-down" capability, which had become standard in American fighters. This made it possible for an American pilot to detect other aircraft from high altitudes, without experiencing interference from the clutter of the earth's surface.

In addition to praising some aspects of the MiG-25's radar for being so powerful, Air Force experts said the aircraft's flight-control computer was also impressive. It not only controlled the sensor systems and the firing of weapons, it returned the plane to any one of four landing fields. The pilot had little to do except guide the plane through its takeoff, wait for the interception of an enemy aircraft (which was controlled from the ground), fire the plane's missiles, and, on return, land the plane. A United States Air Force officer called the system "the most sophisticated ever in a modern plane."

But the plane also showed signs of poor workmanship. The welding and riveting were sloppily done. Fatigue cracks in parts of the airframe had been repaired with rough welds. The body and wings were marked with spots of brownish rust.

But these failings had little to do with the Foxbat's flight capability. "We thought it was a damned good plane and that's what it turned out to be," said another Air Force official. "We're not belittling it because it rusts. In fact, it can fly higher, faster, and with a bigger payload than any plane in the world."

Like the MiG-23 that preceded it, the MiG-25 was produced in many different versions. They include:

MiG-25, Foxbat A—The basic interceptor with the primary mission of attacking high-flying targets.

MiG-25R, Foxbat B—The basic reconnaissance version.

MiG-25U, Foxbat C—Trainer version with separate cockpit and canopy.

MiG-25R, Foxbat D—A second reconnaissance version with improved radar.

MiG-25M, Foxbat E—Interceptor similar to MiG-25, Foxbat A, with improved radar providing limited look-down, shoot-down capability, a sensor mounted beneath the nose and upgraded engines.

MiG-25, Foxbat F—Equipped with antiradar missiles to attack surface-to-air missile sites. Entered service in 1986.

The fact that the MiG-31 Foxhound, which began to be deployed in 1983, closely resembles the MiG-25 is no accident. The two planes have virtually the same airframe. The MiG-31 is a much different aircraft, however. A long-rage interceptor with a two-man crew, the MiG-31 can

The MiG-31 Foxhound, a long-range interceptor that was introduced in 1983, has the same air frame as the MiG-25. (U.S. Navy)

outrun almost anything else in the sky. Armed with giant missiles similar to the Phoenix, the plane can attack ground targets from any altitude.

In total, the Soviet Union produced less than 1,000 MiG-25s, a low production for a Soviet fighter. Several thousand MiG-23s were turned out, and over 20,000 MiG-21s.

During the 1990s, most MiG-25s continued to serve the Soviet Union as strategic interceptors and reconnaissance planes. Foxbats were also in use with the air forces of Algeria, India, Iraq, Libya and Syria.

7 F-15 EAGLE

The first F-15s to go into service in 1974 were air-to-air fighters. As a big, highly maneuverable missile carrier with Mach 2.5 speed, the plane ruled the skies. No other fighter could out-climb or out-accelerate it. In mock combat drills against Soviet MiGs, the F-15 almost never failed to win.

F-15 fighters on a training mission over Luke Air Force Base near Phoenix, Arizona. (McDonnell Douglas Corporation)

F-15 FACT SHEET

Manufacturer: McDonnell Aircraft Company

Type: Single- or twin-seat fighter with attack capability

Engines: Two Pratt and Whitney F100-PW-100 turbofans, each delivering 24,000 lb. of thrust

Crew: Pilot only or pilot and weapons system officer

Length: 63 ft., 9 in.

Height: 18½ ft.

Wingspan: 42½ ft.

Loaded Weight: 42,300 lb.

Maximum Speed: Mach 2.5+

First Flight: July 27, 1972

But the United States Air Force kept giving the F-15 additional missions, loading the plane with sophisticated guidance and bombing equipment so the plane could fly in all weather, carrying out low-level bombing attacks deep in enemy territory. The latest model, the F-15E, packs a guidance and target-seeking system with a $4 billion price tag. That shot up the cost of just one F-15 to $42 million, which was too much for Secretary of Defense Richard Cheney. He proposed ending the production of the plane after 1991.

A twin-engine, fixed-wing aircraft, the F-15 is easy to spot because of its twin tails, large canopy, and delta (or triangular-shaped) wing. It is also very big for a fighter. Some say it is too big. Its critics call the F-15 the "twin-tailed tennis court" or "Rodan," the name of a Japanese flying monster.

The F-15 is a thrill to fly. Although the plane's fuselage-mounted, turbofan, afterburning engines produce speeds in excess of Mach 2, the F-15 can also maintain controlled flight at less than 100 knots (115 miles an hour).

Each engine produces 24,000 pounds of thrust. Because the total thrust is greater than the aircraft's weight (42,300 pounds)—a first for any American fighter—the F-15 can climb straight up at incredible speed.

A specially prepared F-15, nicknamed the "Streak Eagle," once took part in a series of demonstration flights in which the plane revved up its engines while stopped dead on the runway, then shot up rocketlike to over 39,000 feet (more than seven miles) in less than one minute. It topped 65,000 feet in just over two minutes. When it stopped climbing, the plane was more than 103,000 feet above the ground. At one time, the F-15 held eight time-to-climb records.

Typical armament for the F-15 consists of four radar-guided, advanced Sparrow missiles, four heat-seeking Sidewinder missiles, and a Vulcan 20-millimeter cannon with 940 rounds of ammunition. In place of the Sparrow and Sidewinder missiles, the F-15 can carry AMRAAM missiles. (AMRAAM stands for advanced, medium-range, air-to-air missile—another weapon that guides itself to the target.)

When it comes to range and the amount of time the aircraft can remain aloft, the F-15 also gets high marks. It has flown five-hour missions without refueling. With aerial refueling, a mission can be stretched to 10 hours.

Today's F-15s carry about 2,000 gallons of fuel in internal tanks. Teardrop-shaped fuel tanks are mounted beneath the fuselage, more than doubling the amount of fuel the plane can carry. (During the early 1990s, it cost about $5,000 to fill the tanks of an F-15 with jet fuel.) An Eagle equipped with external fuel tanks has flown nonstop from the United States to Europe without refueling.

Underside view of F-15 Eagles reveals Sidewinder and Phoenix missiles.
(McDonnell Douglas Corporation)

The F-15's high-power radar offers a detection range of over 100 miles. It can detect and track targets at all altitudes, both above and below the aircraft. When "looking down," many radars have difficulty distinguishing the target from the ground because of interference, called ground clutter. But the F-15's radar features clutter-free, lock-on tracking and missile guidance.

Also aboard is a system that overcomes jamming signals broadcast by enemy aircraft and meant to confuse the Eagle's radar. The F-15 can outjam the jammers, in other words.

While today's fighters are much more complex than those of the past, they are not any more difficult to fly. That's because many of the chores that have to do with communication, navigation and the monitoring of weapon systems have been taken over in whole or in part by onboard computers.

Pilots of the F-15 and other, late-model combat aircraft benefit from HUD, or head-up display. HUD takes the form of a small sheet of glass that is mounted just above the forward instrument panel. Onto it are projected navigational and weapons-related information. At the same time that he is reading such vital information as heading, airspeed, altitude and angle of attack, the pilot never has to avert his eyes from the view ahead.

In designing cockpit interiors, the U.S. Air Force follows a philosophy called HOTAS, for hands on throttle and stick. It dictates that the pilot's hands should never have to leave the throttle or stick, which controls the aircraft's speed and power; nor should his eyes ever have to look down or back into the cockpit.

At one time, it was discovered that the positioning of a radio panel in the cockpit of the F-4 was contributing to accidents after takeoff. The pilot was forced to bend his head down in order to change radio frequencies. On today's aircraft, the radio-frequency selector is placed high and forward, just underneath the HUD. The other switches and knobs in the cockpit are all distinctively shaped, so that the pilot can tell by feel which is which.

The original model of the F-15, the F-15A, was a one-seat plane. So is the F-15C. But the F-15B, F-15D and F-15E are two-seaters. These models have the same appearance as the single-seat Eagles, except for a slightly larger canopy.

In the U.S. Air Force, the man who rides behind the pilot is called the weapons system officer—WSO. (In the Navy, this specialist is designated as the radar intercept officer—RIO.) WSOs—or "whizzos," as they've been nicknamed—are not copilots, even though their controls include a flight stick and other systems that enable them to fly the plane from the back seat. It's always the pilot who flies the plane. The WSO operates the radio, monitors the radar, and, in combat, keeps on the lookout for enemy aircraft.

Air Force pilots have had a variety of nicknames for the man in the rear seat. Popular during the Vietnam War was GIB, short for "guy in back." The WSO has also been known as an "ace of gauges," "scope dope" or "gator," a shortened version of navigator.

Because the rear seat has restricted vision, it is sometimes referred to as the pit. This has led to the back seat occupant being called the "pitter" or "prisoner of the pit."

At most Air Force bases around the world, a pilot and his WSO usually learn of any mission in which they are to take part the day before, when information about the next day's operations are posted. They're told their takeoff time and the type of mission it is to be.

About two hours before takeoff, crew members attend a flight briefing, a kind of mission-planning session. The flight leader, usually the pilot to fly the first aircraft, conducts the briefing.

During the briefing, which lasts about an hour, pilots learn how they will taxi and take off, and how the flight will check in by radio. They get detailed weather information.

The flight leader discusses the type of mission it's going to be. If it's a training mission, he designates who will be the "bad guys" and the "good guys." He explains the types of ordnance that will be used. (Planes never carry live ordnance on training missions.)

After the briefing, the crew suits up and the men head out for their aircraft. Although each squadron has specific planes assigned to it, pilots do not. The plane a pilot flies on a particular mission is a matter of chance. The maintenance crews ready the planes one by one, and the pilot simply takes the next available aircraft.

Before the pilot climbs into the cockpit, he "preflights" the plane. This means he makes a visual inspection of it, checking it against maintenance records.

About 30 minutes before takeoff, the flight leader requests clearance to start the engines. The pilot pulls a handle in the lower right side of the instrument panel, starting a third jet engine that is mounted below and between the F-15's two main engines. This small, auxiliary engine provides electrical power and some hydraulic power for the aircraft. It also powers the pilot's intercom system.

After some preliminary checks, the pilot starts the main engines with the auxiliary engine (in much the same way a car's engine is started by its battery). As soon as the main engines have been started, the auxiliary engine is switched off.

The pilot closes the canopy. He then runs through a series of checks with the crew chiefs, testing the flaps, brakes and other control systems. They also test the various electronic systems, using BIT checks—that is, the built-in-test equipment common to each one.

The pilot also sets up the plane's INS—internal navigation system—which is mounted on the instrument panel. The pilot punches into it the plane's latitude and longitude, and other navigational information concerning the mission. The INS is capable of "remembering" a dozen or so different pieces of information. On a long flight, the pilot would enter each turning point on the flight, as well as important geographic points.

About 10 minutes after the engines have been started, members of the flight check in on the squadron's radio frequency, or "freak," as the pilots call it. The flight leader determines when a pilot is ready to go.

The planes taxi to an area just off the runway for a final inspection. (It's called an "end-of-runway" inspection.) A maintenance crew looks over each aircraft for leaks or other problems that might have developed since the plane was warmed up and taxied.

The plane pulls onto the runway. In clear weather, the aircraft take off in formation. When the weather is bad, they take off one by one, 20 seconds apart. Each aircraft has a radar lock-on to the aircraft in front.

The seats in an F-15 are tilted back at a 30-degree angle. It's something like sitting at a desk with your feet up. This positioning puts each crew member's head more in line with his heart, which helps his body to better withstand the G-forces experienced at high speeds.

Because of its size—its large wing surface, in particular—the F-15 can cope with more G's than most aircraft. A "G" is the normal force of gravity—a unit equal to the gravity exerted on a body at rest. At one G, a 200-pound man weighs 200 pounds. At four G's, he weighs 800 pounds.

In a speeding airplane, G forces vary widely as the plane maneuvers in the sky. They are the greatest when the plane pulls out of a dive or makes a right turn. In tests, the F-15 has shown that it can withstand as many as nine G's.

In a nine-G turn, the pilot experiences pressure that is nine times the weight of gravity, meaning that a 200-pound pilot will feel like he weighs 1,800 pounds, almost a ton (2,000 pounds). He will have trouble lifting his arms or tilting back his head. The flesh on his face will feel like it's rubbery and melting.

In a very-high-G turn or dive, the pilot's blood could rush away from his brain, causing him to black out. A G-suit helps to prevent this.

The G-suit is an inflatable harness that wraps around the pilot's legs and hips like a pair of trousers. Connected to the aircraft's pressure system and "G-meter," the G-suit automatically squeezes the pilot's lower body during high-pressure maneuvers and keeps the blood from draining to his feet.

Another problem caused by G forces are the reddish blotches that appear on the pilot's bodies. These result from a rupturing of small blood vessels, called capillaries. The red marks appear on the buttocks, bellies and under the arms of the pilot and the WSO. Crew members call them "high-G measles" or "fighter hickeys."

During the Korean War, from 1950 to 1953, the F-86 Sabre was a star performer, enjoying extraordinary success against Soviet-built MiG-15s. The F-86 looked like what a fighter was supposed to look like. It had a swept-back wing and a high cockpit with outstanding visibility for the pilot. It also had superior maneuverability.

According to Air Force records, of the 839 MiGs destroyed in combat in Korea, 800 were brought down by F-86 Sabres. Only 58 F-86s were lost in action. No wonder the F-86 is looked upon, along with the P-51 Mustang of World War II, as one of the greatest fighters.

In the years that followed the Korean War, aircraft designers failed to follow up on the success of the F-86. They got sidetracked. Instead of developing true fighters, they became involved with the array of electronics and missiles that had become available. Future battles in the sky—"dogfights," as they were called—would be fought without ever seeing the enemy. Or so it was believed.

The first opportunity for aircraft to use the new technology came during the Vietnam War. The results were disappointing. The fact that the new electronics and missiles were often unreliable was only part of the problem. There simply were no aircraft available with superior air-to-air, all-weather capabilities.

There were fighter-bombers, such as the F-4, F-100 and F-105. There were interceptors—the F-102, F-104 and F-106. But there was no classic fighter in the tradition of the F-86 Sabre or P-51 Mustang.

What fighter pilots were asking for was a plane with greater agility at medium and low altitudes. Speed alone wasn't enough. The ability to accelerate, to climb and dive, to be able to get the best angle on the enemy, and get it fast, was what was needed.

Late in 1968, eight companies were invited to submit design proposals for the new aircraft. Only four of the eight did. In December 1969,

McDonnell Douglas's design was selected. Contracts for the production of the first aircraft were issued.

The new plane could have been designated the F-13, which was the next available number. Earlier, the Navy had skipped 13 when choosing a number for its new fighter, calling it the F-14. Superstition was undoubtedly the reason. The Air Force decided to pass over 13, too. The plane would be known as the F-15.

The first 20 aircraft produced were used for testing. When it came to evaluating the qualities that go toward making for air superiority, F-15s were pitted in one-to-one engagements against a wide variety of aircraft flown by highly skilled Air Force pilots. The flights were conducted over the test range at China Lake, California. The results startled observers:

In 46 engagements with T-38 jet trainers, which were simulating the MiG-21, the F-15 won every battle.

In 29 engagements against the F-5E fighter, which also simulated the MiG-21, the F-15 won every time.

In 17 engagements against the A-4, simulating a MiG-17, the F-15 won every time.

In 13 engagements against the F-106, simulating a MiG-23, the F-15 won every time.

In four engagements against the A-37 attack aircraft, the F-15 won every time.

In 69 engagements against F-4 Phantoms, which simulated the MiG-23, the F-15 won 67.

The test series ended after 178 engagements. The F-15 won 176 of them.

The Air Force began taking delivery of the F-15 in November 1974. The original plan was to buy 729 planes. But the number actually purchased has gone well beyond 1,000. The F-15 has proven popular not only with Air Force officials but with several foreign countries as well, including Saudi Arabia, Japan and Israel.

The Israeli assortment of some 50 Eagles includes F-15s of every model. In June 1979, a handful of Israeli F-15s clashed with Syrian Air Force MiGs over southern Lebanon. It marked the first time that an advanced U.S. jet aircraft had been flown in combat. The F-15s' opponent that day, the MiG-21, was a small, light interceptor, with a maximum speed of Mach 2.1, but only above 30,000 feet. At low altitudes, its maximum speed was Mach 1.06.

The MiG-21 was usually armed with two infrared homing missiles, similar to the American-made Sidewinder missile, plus two rocket packs, each with 16 57-millimeter rockets. The F-15 carried four radar-guided Sparrow missiles, which have a greater range than the infrared homing type.

A pair of F-15 Eagles fly over Hohenzollern Castle, south of Stuttgart, Germany. (U.S. Department of Defense)

The clash left no doubt as to the superiority of the F-15. Israel said that its pilots shot down at least four of the Syrian aircraft. All of Israel's F-15s returned safely to the base.

The Royal Saudi Air Force purchased 46 F-15Cs and 16 F-15Ds in 1981. In June 1984, Saudi F-15s shot down a pair of Iranian fighter planes over the Persian Gulf. The downed planes, through a strange twist of events, were F-14 Phantom IIs. They had been purchased by the Iranian government from McDonnell Douglas, the manufacturer.

Japan has purchased 187 F-15s for its Japanese Air Self-Defense Force. Of that number, 173 of the aircraft will be built in Japan.

One reason foreign countries like the F-15 is because it is easy to maintain and keep in operation. A fighter that cannot fly cannot fight.

At the first hint of trouble, the aircraft is grounded and the engine is pulled out. A maintenance crew can change an F-15's engine in an hour and a half. The faulty engine is then examined until the source of the problem is found.

If the problem has to do with the fighter's electronics and avionics, they're designed to slide easily in and out of the aircraft. The obvious advantage of this is in keeping the plane fully mission-capable, because malfunctioning parts can be replaced quickly and easily. And the job doesn't require someone with a great deal of special training. If you can change the battery in a family automobile, you can probably install a black box. And black boxes can be shuttled around from one aircraft to another with little trouble.

But one problem with black boxes is that they must be taken to special shops with the right kind of equipment for repairs. On the old F-4s, fixing the radio was a complex piece of business. Still, a skilled and persistent maintenance crew could do it. But there's no repairing the radio on an F-15—unless you have the right black box.

The very latest Eagle is the F-15E, a high-speed, long-range, all-weather fighter and interceptor—an aircraft capable of either high-altitude or low-altitude penetration and attack. The plane can carry 12 tons of missiles and bombs.

The first prototypes of the F-15E were flown in December 1986. The first operational versions of the plane were assigned to the Fourth TFW (Tactical Fighter Wing) at Seymour Johnson Air Force Base, Goldsboro, North Carolina. By the beginning of 1991, slightly more than 100 F-14Es were on active duty.

The Air Force planned to have a total of 1,074 F-15s in operation by the mid-1990s. This figure does not include the first 20 Eagles, which were used for testing and development.

Yet another version of the Eagle, now being tested, is something of a dream machine. It combines the tremendous speed and maneuverability of the standard version of the F-15 with the ability to make short takeoffs and landings. Flight trials for the new aircraft, designated F-15 S/MTD (STOL/maneuvering technology demonstration), began in September 1988 and continued into the 1990s.

The short-takeoff-and-landing (STOL) Eagle has engines that are similar in concept to those of the AV-8B Harrier. They take air, compress it and blast it through nozzles angled downward to give vertical lift, or directed backward to send the aircraft forward at supersonic speed.

Right now, however, the United States Air Force is perfectly happy with existing models of the F-15. The best indication of the Air Force's high regard for this aircraft came in the summer of 1990, when military forces commanded by Iraq's President Saddam Hussein overran Kuwait, plunging the Persian Gulf region into crisis.

U.S. President George Bush ordered American troops, armor, and jet fighters and bombers to Saudi Arabia. Forty-five F-15s were among the first aircraft to be deployed—the First Tactical Fighter Wing with its F-15Bs and F-15Cs, and the Fourth Tactical Fighter Wing, equipped with F-15Es. Reliable and versatile, the F-15s were trusted to fend off any threat to Saudi Arabia and its neighbors.

On January 16, 1991, when the United States went to war against Iraq, F-15s were among the first planes to see action, bombing strategic and military targets in the city of Baghdad. In the days that followed, F-15s played a vital role in helping allied forces gain control of the skies.

Some Arab pilots flew F-15s during the conflict. One day late in January, a flight of Iraqi F-1 Mirage fighters were spotted on allied radar screens. Capt. Ayed al-Shamrami of the Royal Saudi Air Force was on patrol in his F-15 that day. He shot down two Mirages and became a national hero.

8   F/A-18 HORNET

This F/A-18 Hornet carries MK-83 bombs and, for defensive purposes, radar-guided Sparrow and heat-seeking Sidewinder missiles. (McDonnell Douglas Corporation)

When designers and engineers set to work to develop the aircraft that was to become the F/A-18 Hornet, they faced an almost impossible task. Their assignment was to design an aircraft that would outdo the much acclaimed F-14 Phantom as a fighter and, at the same time, surpass the A-7 Corsair, the workhorse bomber of the Vietnam War, as an attack plane. The aircraft also had to be sophisticated enough to be able to serve the air wings of the Navy and Marine Corps well into the 21st century.

F/A-18 FACT SHEET

Manufacturer: McDonnell Aircraft Company

Major Subcontractor: Northrop Corporation

Type: Carrier- or land-based fighter and attack aircraft.

Engines: Two General Electric F404-GE-400 turbofans, each delivering 16,000 lb. of thrust

Crew: Pilot only

Length: 56 ft.

Height: 15 ft,. 3½ in.

Wingspan: 40 ft, 4¾ in.

Loaded Weight: 56,000 lb.

Maximum Speed: Mach 1.7+

First Flight: June 9, 1974

What resulted from their efforts is the F/A-18, an aircraft that its principal manufacturer, the McDonnell Douglas Corporation, calls a strike fighter. It's a single-seat, twin-engine, exceptionally maneuverable plane that can be used on aircraft carriers or ashore at shore stations.

The F-4 Phantom and F-14 Tomcat are faster than the F/A-18 (the "F" is for fighter, "A" for attack). Each can get to its destination quicker than the F/A-18 can. But once there, they can be handicapped by a lack of maneuverability. Turning is a cumbersome process. The F/A-18, on the other hand, can turn on a dime.

The most violent maneuver possible in the F/A-18 (is what pilots call a break turn. It's used when cockpit instruments tell the pilot that an enemy is firing at him. Then he actually sees the missiles coming, thick trails of white smoke headed toward him. He pulls hard on the stick. Instantly the nose shoots up, taking the plane out of the missile's projected path.

The Hornet can carry up to 17,000 pounds of ordnance beneath the fuselage and wing. For air-to-air combat, the F/A-18 carries two radar-guided Sparrow missiles, mounted at the lower end of the fuselage, and two heat-seeking Sidewinder missiles under the wing. The Hornet was the first Navy aircraft flying in fleet operations to be armed with advanced, medium-range, air-to-air missiles (AMRAAM). The F/A-18's armament also incudes a 20-mm cannon.

For air-to-ground missions, the Hornet keeps its Sidewinders and cannon for its own defense. Infrared and laser-targeting sensors replace the fuselage-mounted Sparrows. These provide information that help in achieving accuracy with the bombs and missiles.

The design of the F/A-18 is based on the YF-17, a test aircraft built by the Northrop Corporation. Northrop spent eight years in developing the YF-17 and claimed no fighter in the world was as maneuverable. Although the plane was never known for its speed, it was exceptional in terms of acceleration, and in climb and turn rate. The YF-17 made its first flight early in 1974.

Northrop had designed the YF-17, not for the Navy but as an Air Force plane, specifically to serve as the Air Force's air-combat fighter of the 1970s and 1980s. General Dynamics was also in the competition with its F-16. When the Air Force picked the F-16 over the YF-17, it was a bitter disappointment for Northrop. It was then that the company looked toward the Navy, which was seeking an aircraft to replace its aging fleet of F-4 Phantoms and A-7 Corsairs. Because Northrop had

A pair of Navy F/A-18s, each armed with heat-seeking Sidewinder missiles and also carrying a 330-gallon external fuel tank. (Mc-Donnell Douglas Corporation)

no recent experience in dealing with the Navy, the company was quick to accept an offer from McDonnell Douglas to team up on the project.

Several important changes had to be made in the YF-17 to make it suitable for carrier operations. The wing area of the plane was increased by some 50 feet. The nose was made bigger to accommodate the larger radar necessary for the Navy's weapons system. The fuselage was lengthened to provide for bigger fuel tanks. Engine power was boosted.

The F/A-18's two General Electric F404 engines are modifications of the YJ101 engines used in Northrop's YF-17, the Hornet's prototype. They each generate approximately 16,000 pounds of thrust, or about 1,000 pounds more thrust than the YJ101.

The engines are efficient, light in weight—and simple. Simplicity in engine design makes for trouble-free operation and easier maintenance. Mechanics can change an engine in the F/A-18 in less than half an hour, or about the same amount of time it takes the average motorist to replace a flat tire.

There are fewer parts in the F404 than in most other high-performance engines. The F404 has about the same amount of thrust as the J79 engine that powers the F-4 Phantom, but the Hornet's engine is half as heavy and has 7,700 fewer parts.

Landing on an aircraft carrier puts tremendous demands on an airplane. There are five arresting wires—or "traps"—that lie across the carrier's deck. The pilot tries to catch the third wire, halfway up the deck, with the plane's tailhook. That's ideal. If he hooks any one of the other four wires, that's OK, too. The plane is brought to an abrupt stop.

Each landing is a touch-and-go operation. As the pilot puts his plane down, he has to be ready to advance the throttle to full power, in case his hook misses all five wires. That means he has to go through the humiliating experience of "bolting," speeding up and hurtling off the deck to go around and try landing again.

The plane has to have plenty of thrust. Otherwise, on a "bolter," it would never be able to get back up into the air again, but would be likely to plunge off the end of the deck. The Navy would not only lose an airplane; the pilot might lose his life.

A plane made for carrier landings and takeoffs has to be able to get up into the air fast. It has to have plenty of lift. Engineers at McDonnell Douglas and Northrop worked to improve the lift characteristics of the F/A-18 by installing extra panels along the front edge of the wing flaps.

The Navy ordered 11 test versions of the new plane early in 1976. McDonnell Douglas was to be the prime contractor, producing the forward fuselage, wings and landing gear. Northrop was to build the rear fuselage and install the plane's engines. Final assembly would take place at the McDonnell Douglas plant in St. Louis.

The first of the versatile, potent Hornets was introduced in September 1978. In its first test flight later that fall, the aircraft performed without a hitch. Jack Krings, chief test pilot for McDonnell Douglas, reported the aircraft was "extremely stable" during its landing approaches, a highly valued feature in a carrier airplane.

In flight testing early in 1979 at the Naval Air Test Center at Patuxent River, Maryland, the Hornet continued to impress observers. Test pilots were delighted with the smooth ride the plane provided at low levels, even in turbulent air. The aircraft never failed to get high marks for its agility. Time after time, it "lost" chase planes that were assigned to monitor its maneuvers.

F/A-18 Hornets prepare to be launched from the deck of the carrier Constellation. (McDonnell Douglas Corporation)

Photographed over the Mediterranean Sea, an underside view of an F/A-18 assigned to the carrier Coral Sea. (U.S. Navy)

In the fall of 1979, the F/A-18 went to sea for the first time. In test flights made from the carrier *America*, the aircraft made 17 touch-and-go landings and 32 cable-arrested landings, and met every expectation.

There were speed tests, too. The Hornet generated Mach 1.6 at 40,000 feet, and Mach 1.5 at 50,000 feet. There were other fighters that could go faster. But the fact that the F/A-18 could turn tighter and climb faster than any enemy plane compensated for its lack of speed.

The Navy ordered 1,366 F/A-18s, despite the fact that the plane had escalated in cost. In fact, the cost of each F/A-18 was, by 1980, within about $2 million of what the F-14 Tomcat cost, and the Tomcat was the Navy's most expensive fighter ever. By the mid-1980s, each F/A-18 was costing the Navy $18 million.

In February 1985, the A-7 fleet squadrons aboard the carrier *Constellation* became the first to trade in their Corsairs for Hornets. One former A-7 pilot said he felt more comfortable in the F/A-18 after 200 hours at the controls than he did in his old Corsair after 2,000 hours.

The United States Marines also fly the F/A-18. Marine squadrons have used the Hornet to replace the F-4.

Canada has purchased 138 Hornets, while Australia has bought 57. These were assembled in Australia, with many of the parts turned out in Australian factories. Spain is another foreign customer, having purchased 72 F/A-18s for use as reconnaissance planes.

One American pilot summed up his experience in the F/A-18 in these words: "I would say it's state of the art. Every aspect of the Hornet represents the best of current technology. The engines put out a tremendous amount of power for their size and weight, and they are reliable. The avionics are futuristic. The weapons system makes aces out of ordinary pilots. The plane is easy to maintain.

"About the only negative is that it isn't cheap. But, then, neither is a Ferrari."

9   *JA37 VIGGEN (THUNDERBOLT)*

To many, Sweden has long represented peace and harmony in a world of turmoil. It offers life without war, without hunger or other serious wants. The Swedish have always seemed to be able to settle their differences in a reasonable way.

But Sweden's geography has been a constant threat to its tranquility. During the Cold War years, Sweden was a buffer state, often a very nervous one. Just to its east are Finland and the Soviet Union. The Warsaw Pact nations lie to the south, just beyond the Baltic Sea. Norway and Great Britain—staunch NATO nations—are to the west. At any moment during those years of tension between East and West, it seemed one superpower conflict or another might spill over onto Swedish soil.

JA37 FACT SHEET

Manufacturer: SAAB, the Swedish Aeroplane Company

Type: All-weather interceptor with attack capability

Engines: One Volvo Flygmotor RM8B turbofan, delivering 16,200 lb. of thrust

Crew: Pilot only

Length: 53 ft., 10 in.

Height: 19 ft., 4 in.

Wingspan: 34 ft., 9 in.

Loaded Weight: 33,000 lb.

Maximum Speed: Mach 2+

First Flight: February 8, 1967

Sweden's chief means of preserving its neutrality during that period was a fighter plane—the mighty SAAB JA37 Viggen (loosely translated, Viggen means thunderbolt). Viggen squadrons stood ready to intercept hostile aircraft or to attack surface targets or ships. They also monitored and reported any naval activity in Swedish waters.

Sweden's JA37 Viggen can operate as an all-weather interceptor or attack plane. (SAAB-Scania; A. Anderson)

The JA37's unique double-delta wing helps the aircraft get into the air fast and land on short runways. (SAAB-Scania; A. Anderson)

The single-seat JA37 is a powerful plane, yet it is also very agile. And, like all Swedish combat aircraft, it's exceptionally rugged.

There's good reason for Swedish ruggedness. Not only must Sweden's combat planes have the ability to operate in the often stormy weather and deep-freeze temperatures of northern Europe—sometimes well within the Arctic Circle—their fighters must also be capable of takeoffs and landings on rough airfields in remote stretches of the country.

Sometimes a landing field will be little more than a straight stretch of unpaved road, or a dirt track. These emergency strips require Swedish fighters to combine supersonic speed with the ability to land perfectly and get up into the air fast.

In the case of the Viggen, Swedish designers might have solved this problem with a variable-swept wing—one that could be fully extended on landings and takeoffs (as with the F-14 Tomcat). The vectored-thrust system (used in the AV-8B Harrier) is another method of getting a plane into the air quickly.

But the engineers at SAAB had yet another idea—a wing system with a unique double-delta shape. The advanced design of the Viggen offers two triangular-shaped wing surfaces, one mounted in front of the other. The foreplane, as it's called, is positioned just ahead of and slightly higher than the much larger main delta.

Both wings are fitted with trailing-edge flaps. Operated together during takeoffs and landings, they generate tremendous lift. This dou-

JA37's heavy duty under-carriage is similar to that used on carrier aircraft. (SAAB-Scania; A. Anderson)

ble-wing feature is one important reason the Viggen is able to get up into the air fast and make landings on very short airstrips.

When landing, the Viggen can be brought in at a speed of less than 140 miles an hour. It's slammed to the ground in much the same way a carrier plane is brought in for a landing. (In fact, the Viggen's undercarriage is similar to that used on carrier aircraft.)

As he eases the plane in, the Viggen pilot gives the engines a full reverse thrust, which brakes the plane even on icy runways.

Thanks to these special features, the Viggen can land on a runway of only 1,600 to 1,700 feet. It can take off in an even shorter distance.

The first discussions concerning the plane that was to become the JA37 Viggen go back to the early 1950s. From the beginning, it was planned that the aircraft would have a multimission role—that it would be capable of replacing not only Sweden's fighters but its attack and reconnaissance planes as well.

A project team at SAAB (an acronym for Svenska Aeroplan Aktiebolag, or the Swedish Aeroplane Company) went to work on the project in 1961. They chose an American-built Pratt and Whitney engine to power the new plane. It was much the same engine used in such commercial airliners as the Douglas DC-9 and Boeing 727. But Sweden's Flygmotor modified the engine so that it would be capable of supersonic speeds. The result was one of the most powerful military jet engines in the world. Today, the Viggen's engines are built in Sweden under a licensing arrangement between Flygmotor and Pratt and Whitney.

It was also decided very early in the planning that computers would control as many systems as possible, including navigation, fuel monitoring and weapons use.

On February 8, 1967, the first Viggen prototype made its first flight. Everything went as planned.

No serious problems developed with the aircraft, in fact, until 1974, long after the first production models had been delivered. Three aircraft were lost in flight for unknown reasons. After long and careful investigation, it was found that cracks had developed in the main wing spar of the first 28 Viggens to have come off the assembly line. This failing had contributed to the crashes. All the planes produced after the first 28 had been fitted with a heavier spar. The heavier spar was then installed on all the remaining earlier planes.

Besides the attack version of the Viggen, SAAB also produced two reconnaissance models and a two-seat trainer. The SF37 photo-reconnaissance plane carried not only advanced camera equipment for day and night photography but Sidewinder missiles for self-defense.

The SH37 is both a reconnaissance and attack plane. Its primary mission is sea surveillance—that is, keeping an eye on naval traffic in waters near Sweden. The aircraft relies on powerful search radar as well as cameras carried in underwing pods for both day and night use. The two-seat SK37 trainer can also be used for attack missions.

Although the Viggen satisfies Sweden's defense needs for the present, an entirely new fighter is planned for the future. It's the SAAB JAS39 Gripen (for "griffin," a fabled monster with the head and wings of an eagle and the body of a lion). Like the Viggen, the Gripen has a double-delta wing.

But there are many differences, including a more powerful engine. Much of the Gripen's airframe is built of high-strength composite materials. The wing, for example, is of carbon-fiber construction. Other composite parts include the vertical tail, nose and all gear doors.

There are some 30 computers in the Gripen. They handle such systems as flight control, environmental control, navigation, fuel and hydraulics.

The Swedish Air Force plans to have 140 Gripens in service by the year 2000. But for the remaining years of this century, Sweden will continue to depend on the powerful Viggen.

10   MiG-29 (FULCRUM)

Only July 1, 1986, much to the surprise of NATO observers, six unarmed but otherwise combat-ready, twin-engine Soviet fighter planes, previously known only from satellite images and a series of takeoff photos, circled the Finnish air base of Kuopio-Rissala, and then landed to begin a goodwill visit. The planes were MiGs, but completely unlike any other fighter ever developed and built by the MiG design bureau. To the Soviets, the new plane was the MiG-29. NATO dubbed it the Fulcrum.

Main landing gear and engine installations of the MiG-29 resemble those of the F-14 Hornet and F-15 Eagle. (U.S. Air Force)

MiG-29 FACT SHEET

Designer: Mikoyan/Gurevich OKB

Type: Multimission fighter and attack aircraft

Engines: Two Tumansky R-33D turbofans, each delivering 18,300 lb. of thrust

Crew: Pilot only

Length: 56 ft., 5¼ in.

Height: 17 ft., ¾ in.

Wingspan: 34 ft., 5 ½ in.

Loaded Weight: 36,375 lb.

Maximum Speed: Mach 2.3

First Flight: 1979

In addition to its mission as a high-altitude fighter, the MiG-29 was also designed to carry out an interceptor role at low altitudes against such strike aircraft as the American F-111 and the Tornado IDS (interdiction strike), a combat aircraft with a variety of roles, built by Great Britain, West Germany and Italy.

A designer for an American fighter manufacturer observed that the Fulcrum seemed to borrow from the best of two American planes, the F-14 Hornet and the F-15 Eagle. The engine installations and the main landing gear resemble those of the F-14. They retract as they do on the F-14, folding forward so that the wheels lie flat inside the wing. The rear half of the MiG-29, with its big engines beneath the wing, looks like the F-15.

For its air-combat role, the MiG-29 is armed with six close-range air-to-air missiles. It also carries a six-barrel 30-mm cannon in its left wing.

In the nose of the MiG-29, there's an array of advanced radar. This includes radar with a look-down, shoot-down capability. There is also a laser rangefinder and an infrared sensor. These can be operated without throwing off detectable radar signals when approaching targets.

A unique feature of the MiG-29 is the use of hinged doors that close over the engine intakes during the takeoffs and landings. When closed, the doors prevent the engines from picking up foreign objects encountered on the runway. At such times, the engines "breathe" through a series of small openings on each side of the fuselage, to the rear of the cockpit and just above the wing.

What's the reason for these safeguards? It's that the MiG-29 often operates on gravel runways. The plane's large tires are further evidence of this. And the Fulcrum's nosewheel is positioned well back from the plane's nose, so that it won't spin gravel into the engine inlets.

Judging from the plane's size and performance, it seemed obvious the MiG-29 was intended to succeed the MiG-21 Fishbed, MiG-23 Flogger and Su (Sukhoi) 15 Flagon as the Soviet Union's all-weather interceptor. Indeed, by the early 1990s, the replacement program was well under way.

When Mikhail Gorbachev took over leadership of the Soviet Union in 1985, he introduced a spirit of *glasnost*—or openness. Thanks to glasnost, Soviet newspapers and television stations began criticizing

Nose of the MiG-29 is fitted out with different types of advanced radar. (U.S. Air Force)

government social policies. Books that had been banned were republished.

Glasnost also came to have an effect upon Soviet military authorities. During the late 1980s and early 1990s, they invited American and Canadian pilots to fly the MiG-29. Such trust and confidence would have been unthinkable in the days before Mikhail Gorbachev.

When a two-seat MiG-29 visited Canada in connection with Airshow Canada (held at Abbotsford, British Columbia, in the summer of 1989) Major Bob Wade, who flew F/A-18s for the Royal Canadian Air Force, was given permission to fly the Soviet plane. Wade sat in the rear seat of the MiG-29, while Valery Menitsky, chief test pilot for the MiG design bureau, was in the front seat. Since Menitsky spoke little English and Wade less Russian, their conversations on the plane's intercom were largely limited to instructions having to do with transfer of control. "Bob pilot," Menitsky would say when he wanted Major Wade to take the controls. "Valery pilot" was the way Wade phrased his instructions to Menitsky.

After takeoff, the pair performed an afterburner climb to 9,000 feet, and Menitsky put the fighter through a series of mild rolls. Wade wanted to try a tail-slide maneuver to see how well the plane handled. Menitsky pulled the nose almost straight up. The MiG-29 rocketed toward the heavens. Then he abruptly reduced power to idle and airspeed to zero. The plane went backward into a tail slide, falling 200 to 300 feet in two or three seconds. Last, the Soviet pilot lit the afterburner and leveled off.

Menitsky then turned the controls over to Wade, and the Canadian pilot tried the tail slide himself a couple of times. "Most fighters will tail-slide without a problem," Wade later told *Aviation Week and Space Technology*. "But the MiG-29's ability to recover with minimum altitude loss was impressive."

Wade and Menitsky also performed several slow-speed loops and rolls. Menitsky executed a 9-G, 360-degree turn. Wade was at the controls for the final turn, and landed the plane.

Afterward, Wade said he was "very impressed" by the MiG-29's performance.

Early in 1990, David M. North, a pilot and editor representing *Aviation Week and Space Technology*, was permitted to fly a MiG-29 from the Kubinka Air Force base near Moscow. Valery Menitsky also accompanied North on his flight.

Like Wade, North was very favorably impressed by the plane. He described it as "an extremely agile aircraft at slow speeds." He said the

MiG-29 "reflects the Soviet design philosophy of simplicity and reliability." He also noted that "in the hands of a skilled pilot, [the plane] is a lethal weapon against comparable Western-built fighters."

A designer representing the MiG bureau once referred to the "substantial growth potential" of the MiG-29. He was right. The single seat MiG-29s seen in Finland in 1986 were merely the first in a long series of aircraft based on the original design. Others include the following:

Fulcrum A—The basic single-seat fighter and attack aircraft.

Fulcrum B—A combat trainer with a second seat in front of the standard cockpit.

Fulcrum C—Similar to the Fulcrum A, but with the top of the fuselage deeply curved behind the cockpit.

Maritime Fulcrum—Similar to the Fulcrum A, but modified for use in takeoff and landing trials aboard the Soviet carrier *Tbilisi* in 1989.

FBW (fly-by-wire) Fulcrum—An experimental MiG-29 with automatic flight controls, flown for the first time in 1989.

There can be no doubt that the MiG-29 is an extremely important aircraft to the Soviet Union. By the early 1990s, more than 500 MiG-29s

By the early 1990s, more than 500 MiG-29s were in service. (U.S. Department of Defense)

were in service with the Soviet Air Force, and deliveries of the plane had already been completed to East Germany, India, Iraq, North Korea, Poland, Syria and Yugoslavia.

11 F-111

"I'd like to believe I'm a fighter pilot, but I'd probably be one of the first to admit it's a bomber airplane," says a member of an F-111 squadron stationed at Lakenheath, a Royal Air Force base north of London. "The

On a training mission out of Edwards Air Force Base, east of Rosamond, California, an F-111 carries B-83 nuclear bomb dummies. (U.S. Air Force)

F-111 FACT SHEET

Manufacturer: General Dynamics Corporation

Type: Attack aircraft

Engines: Two Pratt and Whitney TF30 afterburning turbofans, each delivering 19,600 lb. of thrust

Crew: Pilot plus weapons system operator

Length: 73 ft., 6 in.

Height: 22 ft.

Wingspan: 31 ft., 11½ in. (swept); 70 ft. (spread)

Loaded Weight: 148,000 lb.

Maximum Speed: Mach 2.5+

First Flight: December 21, 1964

plane was built to do all missions, but it soon became apparent it could not do all missions well, although it could do a couple of missions very well."

One mission the F-111 does very well is interdiction. That's the word military experts use to describe the task of penetrating deep behind enemy lines to bomb supply dumps, ground installations and communication facilities. Put briefly, the F-111, to quote an Air Force official, can "go in."

When trouble flared in the Persian Gulf region in August 1990, and military installations in Iraq loomed as possible targets for American aircraft, the F-111 was one of the first airplanes to swing into action. Fourteen F-111s based in Great Britain were quickly shifted to Incirlik Air Base near Adana, Turkey, 425 miles from Iraq's border.

When the war began between the United States and Iraq in January 1991, F-111s proved to be more effective than almost any other aircraft in carrying out deep strikes. The plane's targets included runways, control towers and fuel and arms depots. F-111s dropped everything from huge cratering bombs to cluster bombs full of grenades or small mines.

One reason the F-111 can perform its mission so well is because of the aircraft's unusual terrain-following capabilities. It swoops toward its target at very low altitudes, beneath enemy radar. With its two-man crew, the plane can operate day or night in all kinds of weather.

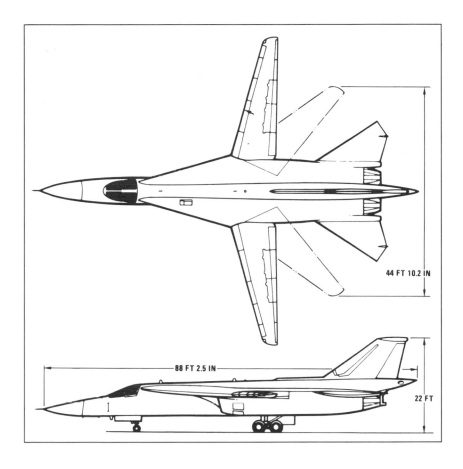

44 FT 10.2 IN

88 FT 2.5 IN

22 FT

That's not the F-111's only unusual feature. It's also the only aircraft in the United States Air Force's arsenal with wings that change position in flight. This enables the plane to take off and land at slow speeds with the wings fully extended, and to fly at more than twice the speed of sound with the wings swept back to form a triangle.

Today, the F-111, which is available in five different versions, is the Air Force's number one attack aircraft, capable of striking any fixed or moving target within a range of well over 1,000 miles, at night or in the worst weather. There's really no other aircraft that can fulfill this mission.

The F-111 has no official nickname. General Dynamics, the plane's manufacturer, calls it simply the F-111 fighter-bomber. In the beginning, General Dynamics wanted to call it the Lancer, but the name never caught on. Australia, the only other nation to operate the F-111, calls its version of the aircraft, the F-111C, the Kangaroo. At various times,

American pilots have dubbed the F-111 the Snoopy, Swinger and Switchblade.

The most popular nickname for the plane is one coined by F-111 pilots in Southeast Asia during the 1970s: the Aardvark. Both the plane and the animal have long snouts. Otherwise, there seems to be no reason to name a fast, high-performance attack aircraft after a large, long-tongued, burrowing animal that feeds on ants and termites. Many of the pilots and WSOs (weapons system operators) who man the plane refer to it by a shortened version of the nickname—the Vark.

"Reagan's Raiders" was a nickname applied to 18 F-111s in 1986. They were the American planes that struck at Libya in April of that year, to punish Libyan leader Col. Muammer el-Qaddafi for sponsoring terrorism.

The raid had its beginnings several months earlier. On December 17, 1985, terrorists preparing to hijack two El Al (Israeli) airliners were spotted by security agents at airports in Rome and Vienna. They reacted by opening fire on passengers in line at El Al ticket counters, killing 20 people, including four Americans.

Afterward, Qaddafi called the killings "heroic actions." He said they demonstrated the "right to export terrorism to America."

In the United States, President Ronald Reagan condemned terrorist missions. He banned trade with and travel to Libya, a sprawling north African nation that is larger than Alaska. Reagan also ordered Americans to leave the country.

But that wasn't all. Orders were relayed to the Deputy Commander at Lakenheath to begin planning for an air strike against the Libyan airfields of Tripoli and Benia, in retaliation for the massacres at Rome and Vienna. The idea was for a small number of F-111s to attack in the middle of the night, relying on surprise for success.

Even for the F-111, one of the world's most advanced aircraft, if not *the* most advanced, the projected mission was especially tough. The long-nosed F-111 normally flew sorties that lasted two or three hours. Going from Lakenheath in England to Libya and back, a distance of about 4,000 miles, would require two or three times as much flying time. But the trip was made even longer when European governments refused to grant permission for the planes to overfly their territory. That meant the F-111s would not be able to fly directly to Libya, Instead, they would have to fly around Portugal and Spain when going and coming. That made it a 6,000-mile journey. The F-111s would have to refuel nine or ten times.

The F-111s based at Lakenheath began secret training missions to the Mediterranean Sea. Not only did the training missions help the pilots to become more skilled in linking up with the KC-10 tankers, they also helped to improve communications and operating procedures with Navy aircraft-carrier battle groups, with whom the raid was to be coordinated.

In the early months of 1986, the likelihood of the attack being carried out rose and fell several times. Late in March, a pair of Libyan surface-to-air missiles fired at two carrier-based American F-14s. The next day, in reprisal, Navy planes sank two French-built Libyan gunboats. Qaddafi sent a message to his "People's Bureaus" throughout Europe the same day, telling them to develop plans for terrorist attacks against Americans.

In April that year, things got even hotter. A bomb exploded in the washroom of La Belle Disco in West Berlin. Two American soldiers and a Turkish woman were victims. Messages were intercepted shortly before and after the bombing between the Berlin People's Bureau and Tripoli, the Libyan capital linking the Libyans to the bombing.

For Ronald Reagan, that was the last straw. He ordered the bombing raid against Libya and Qaddafi, who he called the "mad dog of the Middle East."

Code-named Eldorado Canyon, the mission got under way on April 14, 1986, when 28 KC-10s and KC-135s of the European Tanker Task Force took off from their bases at Mildenhall and Fiarford in England. They were to provide the seven million pounds of fuel the F-111s would require for the mission.

Soon after, the tankers were joined by 24 F-111s from Lakenheath and five reconnaissance F-111s from Upper Heyford. After the first refueling, six F-111s returned to their base. They were to serve as backups, in case one or more of the other planes encountered mechanical difficulties or other problems.

Through the black, moonless night, the F-111s and their tankers sped toward their targets. Three F-111s were assigned to each tanker. One flew behind the tanker, while the others took up positions on each wing.

The planes took on fuel again off the coast of Portugal, south of Spain, and then west of Sicily. Each of the KC-10s was refueled by the bigger KC-135s.

The raid was closely coordinated from the beginning with Navy ships and planes. One the way to the target, the F-111s received intelligence information from the Navy E-2C Hawkeyes, which are equipped with large and very powerful radars, and a Navy cruiser with the Aegis air defense system. A-7 Corsair attack aircraft from the carrier *America* used HARM anti-radiation missiles to destroy air-defense radars. The F-111s were protected by carrier-based F-14 Tomcats, in case Libyan MiGs managed to get airborne to strike at the attackers.

The F-111 air crews had been given some ground rules: All targets had to be positively identified before any ordnance could leave the aircraft. And each plane was given only one chance to hit its assigned target—that is, only one pass was authorized. (Five of the 18 F-111s that made the trip did not drop any bombs.)

Not long before 2:00 A.M., some seven hours after takeoff, the 18 F-111s streaked across the Libyan coast at 540 miles an hour, sweeping over the countryside at an altitude of only 200 feet. Two groups of six planes turned sharply to the left, toward the Sidi Bilal naval base and training center and the Bab al Aziziya barracks, where Qaddafi lived. The remaining planes swung to the south to attack a military airfield at Tripoli, Libya's capital.

As they got closer to their targets, the F-111s climbed to 500 feet so their electronic aiming devices could locate their targets. When the lasers found the range, the WSO in each plane held the target in the crosshairs of an infrared scope. At the last split second, each pilot eased back on his stick, raising the nose of his plane. As bursts of antiaircraft fire began to fill the sky, the WSO sent the bombs toward their target.

The planes that struck the Tripoli airfield destroyed a Soviet-built transport plane and damaged three others. The Sidi Bilal naval base got battered. One of the bombs fell just short of Qaddafi's house, reportedly killing his 15-month-old daughter and injuring two of his sons. Bombs from one of the planes missed Qaddafi's compound entirely, landing near the French embassy in Tripoli. The Libyans said that 37 people died in the attack and 93 were injured.

The raid was over in 12 minutes. One F-111 was lost. It may have been brought down by antiaircraft fire. An extensive search failed to spot the plane or either of its two crew members.

Early the next morning, the raiders returned to Lakenheath, some having been in the air 14 hours. One plane dropped off on the way back, setting down in Spain with engine problems.

The F-111s had performed impressively, although no one took any bows for precision bombing. Starting from airfields in Great Britain, coordinating their mission and its objectives with carrier-based planes in the Mediterranean, the F-111s had carried out the attack with near perfect timing. The crewmen were singled out for special praise. "No matter how much equipment you've got," said Admiral William Crowe, chairman of the Joint Chiefs of Staff, "it still takes a lot of guts to keep that aircraft steady and line up the cross hairs when all kinds of stuff is coming up around you."

The story of the F-111 dates to 1961, when John F. Kennedy became president. To fill his cabinet and many other top-level government positions, Kennedy brought with him a number of reportedly brainy and energetic young men. One was Robert McNamara, Kennedy's secretary of defense.

According to one story, McNamara, when he went aboard an aircraft carrier for the first time, was puzzled by the great array of aircraft. "What good are all those different kinds of planes?" McNamara asked. He believed a good deal of Defense Department money could be saved if the Navy and Air Force used one type of aircraft that would be capable of performing several different missions. The concept was called "commonality."

High-ranking officers from both the Air Force and Navy said it wasn't possible to produce a plane that would satisfy the needs of both services. But McNamara swept all arguments aside, saying that they were the product of service rivalry. The defense secretary set the wheels in motion for the production of the TFX (Tactical Fighter Experimental), as the project was called.

The TFX was doomed from the beginning. The fighter the Navy wanted was a fleet-defense aircraft—a fast, maneuverable dogfighter, but one with the capability of firing long-range missiles to protect carrier task forces from cruise missiles.

The Air Force had an entirely different set of demands. The Air Force wasn't interested in defense. The Air Force wanted a plane that could deliver ordnance. They wanted a strike-and-interdiction aircraft that could operate in all kinds of weather. Pure and simple, the Air Force wanted a bomber.

Despite the different requirements, the project moved ahead. The Air Force's version was designated the F-111A, the Navy's version, the F-111B.

General Dynamics rolled out the first F-111A on October 15, 1964. By this time, President Kennedy had been killed by an assassin's bullet, and Lyndon Johnson, Kennedy's vice president, had advanced to the presidency. But Robert McNamara was still secretary of defense. At the rollout ceremony, McNamara declared: "For the first time in aviation history, we have an airplane with the range of a transport, the carrying capability and endurance of a bomber, and the agility of a fighter-pursuit plane."

In describing the plane, McNamara had fudged a bit. Any major transport plane then in service, including the C-124 and C-135, had far greater range than the F-111A. And two bombers, the B-52 and B-58, could fly farther, too. And there were indeed fighters—the F-106 Delta Dart, to name one—that had greater agility.

One aspect of the F-111 was quite spectacular, however. It was the first combat aircraft of swept-wing design. The wings of the plane rotate on massive hinges, permitting the pilot to actually redesign the shape of the aircraft in flight. On takeoffs and landings, when a large surface is needed to generate lift, wings are fully extended. Relatively short takeoff and landing runs are thus made possible.

Once the plane is airborne and the pilot wants more speed, he sweeps the wings back, reducing lift and drag.

In January 1967, the first fatal accident involving a F-111A took place. Pilot error was said to be the reason. The pilot attempted a landing with the wings set incorrectly. When he realized his mistake and attempted to correct the setting, he moved the wings in the wrong direction. The aircraft plowed into the ground short of the runway.

This was no isolated incident. There were a number of other crashes involving the aircraft in those early days. Criticism was heaped upon the plane.

One set of problems concerned its Pratt and Whitney TF30 engine. As is the case with almost all modern-day fighters, the engines are turbofans. In a turbofan engine, large fans are mounted inside the front of a basic jet engine—also called a turbojet. The fans pull in enormous amounts of air, which cuts down on the amount of fuel the engine uses. Turbofan engines are also quieter.

What was unusual about the engine in the F-111 was that it was the first turbofan to be fitted with an afterburner, the device used to boost an engine's power by burning additional fuel with the exhaust gases. As with any new mechanism, there were unforeseen difficulties. Engine problems played a role in several of the F-111 crashes. Changes had to be made in the engine and the design of its air-intake system.

Eventually, 141 F-111As were produced by General Dynamics. The Air Force rushed six of them to Vietnam in a program called Combat Lancer, which was a disaster. Three of the six aircraft were lost almost immediately. The Air Force grounded the other planes to investigate the cause of the losses.

After the plane returned to the air, the crashes resumed. When the 15th F-111 went down in December 1969, the Air Force again grounded the aircraft. Fatigue cracks were found in the hinges that the wings swing upon. The plane did not go back into service until the problem was corrected.

In September 1972, F-111As returned to Southeast Asia and saw action over North Vietnam as well as Laos. Time and time again, F-111As pounded Hanoi and Haiphong.

They bombed their targets alone, at night and in the worst of weather. Indeed, the plane made strikes in weather so foul that all other aircraft were grounded.

F-111As flew nearly 3,000 missions in Vietnam before the Paris peace accords were signed in January 1973. By that time, The F-111A had won a good many friends.

The F-111B, the Navy's version of the plane, to be built by Grumman, had its own set of problems. The most critical one was getting the big plane down to the Navy's weight limits. The aircraft underwent one weight-reduction program after another.

The canopy was another serious problem. The canopy had to be redesigned because the original one didn't provide the two crew members, sitting side by side, with enough visibility when attempting carrier landings.

Once these modifications were made, the F-111B didn't much resemble the F-111A any more. McNamara's plan to have the Navy and Air Force use the same plane was being swept away.

Problems continued with the F-111B. Three were involved in crashes. Two of these were total losses.

In August 1968, the F-111B program was canceled. That was OK with Grumman. The company could now devote all of its attention to the F-14 Tomcat, a fighter that fulfilled the Navy's requirements—and no one else's.

It wasn't until relatively recent times that the Air Force finally got the airplane it wanted from the beginning—an all-weather attack aircraft. That concept is represented by the F-111E and F-111F, the last-named being the plane that bombed Libya.

The F-111E is an improved version of the F-111A. It has engines that are slightly more powerful. The F-111E was first flown on August 20, 1969. Today, the majority of the F-111Es serve with the 20th TFW (Tactical Fighter Wing) at Upper Heyford, England.

The F-111C is an F-111A built for the Royal Australian Air Force. The Kangaroo, as the Australians have nicknamed the aircraft, has slightly longer wings than the F-111A, and stronger landing gear and brakes.

The F-111D followed the F-111E into service with the U.S. Air Force. Ninety-six were built. The aircraft featured improved electronics

Artist's depiction of the F-111 stresses the plane's bomb-carrying capability.
(General Dynamics)

and an engine with greater power. The F-111D went into operation in November 1971 with the 27th TFW at Cannon Air Force Base near Clovis, New Mexico. It remains the only wing to operate the F-111D.

The F-111F represented another step ahead. It has improved avionics and a yet more powerful engine. One hundred and six F-111Fs were produced. Most are stationed at the 48th TFW at Lakenheath, England. The planes gave up their 20-mm cannons to make room for the PAVE TACK, an all-weather, laser-guided weapons-delivery system. Once its gun was gone, the F-111 could hardly be designated a fighter any more.

Fighter-bomber F-111s can be equipped with a wide variety of ordnance. Although "iron bombs," the high-explosive weapons that go off on impact, are still in use, they are overshadowed by air-to-surface missiles, such as the Harpoon, Maverick and Phoenix. These are homing missiles. They are launched by the F-111 in the general direction of the target. As they near it, the missile's own sensors take over and guide it the rest of the way.

Such missiles are expensive. One version of the Maverick, meant for use against tanks, cost $440,000 apiece during the mid-1980s. At that time, tanks cost only about two or three times that amount.

Air-to-surface missiles can also be anti-radiation missiles. Operated by a computer aboard the aircraft, the ARM homes in on enemy radar transmitters. The HARM and Shrike missiles are two examples of ARM missiles.

Guided missiles, another type of ordnance, are controlled from the aircraft by a TV camera in the missile itself. The operator, watching a TV screen, flies the missile to its target. Or he can get the target on the TV screen, and then the missile-guidance system homes in on it. Some versions of the Maverick are guided missiles.

Iron bombs of the type used in World War II come in an array of sizes, weighing from a few pounds to a ton or more. Some bombs, called "smart" bombs, are similar to guided missiles. Used with great success in the Persian Gulf war, they are guided by a laser beam or other aid focused at the target. This enables the pilot to hit a difficult target without having to get too close to it—that is, to within the range of antiaircraft fire.

Cluster bomb units (CBU) were widely used during the Vietnam War and the Persian Gulf war. Each is a container filled with smaller bombs. When the container hits the ground, it breaks open and flings the smaller bombs over a wide area. A 600-pound CBU contains 150 three-pound bombs.

The smaller bombs can carry different loads, depending on the target. There are antitank loads and incendiary loads. The bombs can also be equipped with timers or sensors. In other words, they can be made to explode at a specific time or when touched.

There is also a completely different F-111, the EF-111A, whose role it is to detect and jam enemy radars. Officially named the Raven, but often referred to as the Electronic Fox because of its EF designation, the EF-111A, introduced in 1981, flies with strike aircraft deep into enemy territory to help prevent them from being detected by electronic air defenses. Four or five Ravens are capable of jamming all of central Europe, stretching from the northern fringe of Poland south to Italy and the Adriatic Sea.

How does one judge the F-111? As an aircraft that was intended to meet the fanciful goals of Secretary of Defense McNamara, the F-111 was a dead failure. When first tried in combat in Vietnam, it failed miserably. But as a strike aircraft able to operate in any kind of weather, it's just what the Air Force ordered. In those terms, the F-111 is an unqualified success.

12   F-16 FIGHTING FALCON

An F-16 armed with Side-winder air-to-air missiles (on the left wing) and an air combat maneuvering instrument pod (on the right wing). (U.S. Air Force)

It was a hot Sunday in June 1981, at Israel's Etzion air base in the Sinai. Out on the flight line, their engines whining, were 14 fighter planes in camouflage colors. Their pilots were the best in the Israeli Air Force, hand-picked for the mission.

The planes consisted of eight F-16s, each carrying two 2,000-pound bombs (a total of 16 tons of TNT), and six F-15s. The F-15s carried

F-16 FACT SHEET

Manufacturer: General Dynamics

Type: Multimission fighter

Engine: One Pratt and Whitney F100-200 turbofan, delivering 23,450 lb. of thrust

Crew: Pilot only

Length: 49 ft., 3 in.

Height: 16 ft., 8½ in.

Wingspan: 32 ft., 9½ in.

Loaded Weight: 37,500 lb.

Speed: Mach 2+

First Flight: January 20, 1974

Sparrow missiles under their fuselages, and Sidewinder missiles and fuel tanks under their wings. The job of the F-15s was to provide a protective mantle for the bomb-laden F-16s.

At 4 P.M., the pilots took off into the blue sky and headed east across Jordan and Saudi Arabia, then plotted a route across the Iraqi desert to Baghdad. Their goal: to destroy Iraq's nuclear reactor at Osirak and its underground facility, where spent nuclear fuel could be converted into plutonium for atom bombs.

For months, the Israeli pilots had been rehearsing for the raid. They had flown countless practice runs over the deserts of Jordan and Saudi Arabia. Their aim was to get used to flying long distances over monotonous desert terrain. Their flights also enabled them to detect "blind" spots in the Jordanian and Saudi radar defenses.

During this time, they also practiced formation flying. The idea was to present a flight pattern that would enable their aircraft to confuse enemy air defenses. Some planes flew singly at very high altitudes. Others stayed very low, close to the desert floor. Still others clustered together. On Iraqi radar screens, they would produce one large blip like that of a commercial airliner, rather than the many tiny blips of approaching fighter planes.

In the final weeks of their training, they practiced bombing runs in the safety of Israeli air space. An actual model of the Osirak reactor was built in the Nagev desert. The Israeli pilots practiced flying in low and releasing their bombs on a flat trajectory toward the target. The idea was to have the bombs knife through the walls of the plant and explode inside.

"Operation Babylon," the secret mission was called. It was scheduled for a Sunday to avoid imperiling the lives of the 150 French and 50 Italian technicians employed at the plant.

The 90-minute flight to Baghdad was tense. While the planes were still over Saudi Arabia, the pilots were suddenly shaken by the voice of an Arab air-traffic controller on their radio frequency. He demanded that the planes identify themselves. An Israeli pilot who spoke Arabic replied that they were Jordanian aircraft on a routine training mission. That seemed to satisfy the questioner, and he signed off.

At 5:30 P.M. the planes approached Baghdad. There was still light enough for them to pick out their target, which was 12 miles south and east of the city. The reactor was ringed by anti-aircraft guns and surface-to-air missiles.

The F-15 interceptors peeled off from the formation and climbed high in the sky to keep guard overhead. The F-16s leveled off at 2,000 feet and lined up to make their bombing runs.

One by one, the little fighters screamed in and dropped their 2,000 pound bombs. Each plane made one pass. Each scored a bull's eye. Within two minutes, it was all over.

There were bursts of flak from the anti-aircraft guns, but none of them hit any of the Israeli planes. No surface-to-air missiles were fired, nor did any Iraqi interceptors take to the air.

On the return flight, the Israeli fighters flew a higher and more direct route that took them over the heart of Jordan. If the Jordanians realized that the Israeli planes had invaded their airspace, they chose to ignore it. The trip back was without incident.

Operation Babylon was a huge success. Videotape recordings made by the pilots showed that the bombs cracked the dome of the reactor like an eggshell, knocking it off its foundation. The reactor core crumbled and collapsed into the cooling pool. And, according to Israel's Prime Minister Menachem Begin, the bombs penetrated all the way into the secret plutonium-processing plant some 12 feet below the ground. "The precision of the bombing was stupefying," a French technician, who had witnessed the raid, told *Newsweek* magazine.

In the war in the Persian Gulf, allied forces gained control of the skies quickly, which enabled military planners to use the F-16 almost exclusively as an attack aircraft. Waves of F-16s and other allied aircraft struck Iraqi targets on a round-the-clock basis.

While capable of Mach 2 speed, the F-16 is also highly maneuverable at low speeds and low altitudes. (General Dynamics)

But strategists ran into a long stretch of bad weather, the worst weather in Iraq and Kuwait in 14 years. The bad weather brought about a change in tactics. A squadron of veteran F-16 pilots, dubbed "Killer Scouts," spotted targets in advance, pointing out to other planes where tanks, artillery and other forces were located. That enabled pilots of other F-16s (and A-10 Thunderbolts) to spend less time looking for targets, and be more effective as a result.

The F-16 is the foremost fighter of the 1990s, the hottest plane in the United States Air Force. It can outfly any other fighter in the world. Its combat range is about 600 miles, although with in-flight refueling it can travel much longer distances. It can carry a bomb load of up to 12,000 pounds. While it is capable of Mach 2 speed, it is also highly maneuverable at low speed and low altitudes.

The F-16 reversed a long-standing trend in the building of fighter aircraft. From the closing stages of World War II and the years of the F-86 Sabre until the mid-1970s and the design and development of the F-15 Eagle, each fighter in turn could fly higher, faster and farther than the one that had preceded it. But as fighter capability increased, so did the fighter size; they kept getting bigger and bigger.

The Vietnam experience showed that big and heavy was not the way to go. Quick and nimble fighters were what was needed to outdo the agile Soviet-built MiGs.

And there was the matter of dollars. Fighters kept costing more, too. The F-15 Eagle was so expensive that it would be virtually impossible to equip every Air Force squadron with it.

What the Air Force wanted was a high-performance, lightweight fighter that could be produced for about $3 million per airframe. Both Northrop and General Dynamics built prototypes for such an airplane. During much of 1973 and all of 1974, the two planes were thoroughly tested. General Dynamics won the competition. In January 1975, the Air Force chose the F-16 as its air combat fighter and placed an order for 650 planes. Although increasing production costs more than doubled and redoubled the plane's price tag, the Air Force eventually ordered a total of 2,609 F-16s. Foreign countries also purchased the plane in sizable quantities.

One of the unusual features of the F-16 is the way in which the pilot's seat is tilted back. It's set at an angle of 30 degrees, which helps the pilot to withstand multiple-G forces.

"The tilt-back seat is just the greatest thing going," says Phil Oestricher, Director of Flight Test for General Dynamics. "Just the other day, I was pulling 9 Gs, and didn't even start to grey out. The reason is the way you sit in the airplane. The heel-rest line is so high that your buttocks are actually the lowest points of your body, and since you are tilted back, the vertical distance from your heart to your brain is also less.

"In all other airplanes, when you pull Gs, the blood tends to pool in your extremities, and the first thing that happens is that you lose vision. In the F-16, the blood flows from your legs down to your posterior, which creates pressure for the blood to return to your heart. It's a kind of neutral G-suit effect.

"The other great thing about the seat position," Oestricher continues, "is the fact that your weight is distributed over a greater area when you're pulling Gs, which makes for less discomfort.

"Then, too, when you're pulling very high Gs, you are in a hard turn and probably looking out the top of the canopy. With your head back against the headrest, you're already looking in the right direction, which makes for fewer knotted neck muscles after the flight."

At the time the first F-16s were built, the plane represented the last word in technological design. The weight of the plane was held in check by the use of advanced aluminum alloys. These were chosen instead of more exotic metals, which can be expensive, to help keep costs down.

The plane offers a computerized flight-control system, or fly-by-wire controls, as they're called. They make maneuvering quick and simple.

Although the Air Force's official name for the F-16 is the Fighting Falcon (the falcon is the mascot of the United States Air Force Academy), pilots who fly the plane called it the Electric Jet. That nickname refers to the aircraft's sophisticated control system.

"If I'm here, and I want to be there, I just sort of *think* there, and I *am* there," says one pilot. "Furthermore, if I want to get from here to there, I just plug in the burner [the afterburner] and point the plane, and I'm there. I don't have to think about accelerating to pick up speed or wait for optimum speed before turning. I just point and I'm gone."

The F-16 gave the Thunderbirds the range to perform for audiences in Western Europe and Africa. Here the demonstration team flies in its diamond formation. (U.S. Air Force)

Flying the F-16 may even be too easy. From the time the first production model took to the air in December 1976 through the early months of 1985, F-16s were involved in nine fatal crashes. The Air Force investigated the accidents, seeking the cause of each.

One theory was that the plane was crashing because of pilot overconfidence. "The airplane gives you a King Kong complex," said one. "A guy stays in the bombing run too long because he knows the F-16 can get him out in a hurry. He eats up his clearances and flies into the ground.

"The airplane makes you feel as if there's nothing you can't do. Even experienced pilots have to be careful that they don't paint themselves into a corner, that they don't get themselves into a situation that even the F-16 can't get them out of."

Like virtually every other military aircraft, the F-16 is subject to constant upgrading. The F-16C, which went into service in 1984, featured many improvements over the earliest version of the aircraft, designated the F-16A. The result was a more powerful and, in many ways, a superior aircraft. For example, the increased structural strength of the F-16C permitted the plane to carry a greater weapons load. New "television screen" cockpit displays placed all kinds of information at the disposal of the pilot, including navigation and weapons data.

General Dynamics has also produced a two-seat version of the F-16, which is used as a trainer. It has been designated the F-16D.

Another version of the F-16 is the F-16XL, a test aircraft. Two prototypes have been built. What makes the F-16XL different is the plane's giant delta-shaped wing. It increase the wing area of the standard F-16 by 155 percent. Since fuel is stored in the wing, the F-16XL provides for an increase in fuel capacity of some 85 percent. There is also room for more electronics.

Thanks to all the fuel it can carry, the F-16XL has almost twice the range of the F-16A. It can also take off and land in about two-thirds of the distance required by the F-16A. If the F-16XL were to go into mass production, it is likely it would be designated the F-16F.

Tomorrow's F-16 is much more likely to be the FSX, for fighter support experimental. A new airplane based on the F-16 design, the FSX is to be a $1.2 billion joint effort between the United States and Japan or, more specifically, General Dynamics and Mitsubishi Heavy Industries.

In making an FSX from the F-16, designers and engineers have proposed increasing the original plane's wing size, using radar-absorbing materials in the leading edge of the wing, adding a drag chute, increasing the length of the nose, adding a small vertical stabilizer (that's mounted to the bottom of the fuselage and is shaped like the keel of a sailboat) and improving the plane's radar, avionic systems, and engine performance.

According to a timetable proposed in 1990, the FSX would be ready for delivery to Japan in 1997. But the arrangement has been hotly opposed by some members of Congress. They say, in helping the Japanese to build the FSX, we'll be giving away important technological secrets. These and other critics say that if the Japanese want an advanced F-16, the United States should build it and sell it to them.

Japan isn't the only foreign country interested in the F-16. Far from it. More than a thousand F-16s have been sold and delivered to foreign air forces. The aircraft is in service in Bahrain, Belgium, Denmark, Egypt, Greece, Indonesia, Israel, the Netherlands, Norway, Pakistan, Singapore, South Korea, Thailand, Turkey and Venezuela.

It's not difficult to understand the popularity of the F-16. Just ask a pilot who has flown the plane. "The thing is really sensational," says one. "I have never experienced anything so responsive, so light on the controls, so positive in its reactions to my control inputs, and yet so reassuringly comfortable to fly."

13 MIRAGE III

During a combat patrol over the Golan Heights, my wingman spotted two Syrian Su-7B strike fighters coming in at 12 o'clock high. A quick warning shout alerted me to the danger, and we prepared to engage them. They barrelled on downwards toward our troop positions, sweeping low over the area, followed closely by a trail of smoke puffs as their rockets exploded on the ground below them. At the end of their run, the two intruders pulled up sharply to gain altitude for another attack. We hit the afterburners and rolled into position behind the Syrian leader, just as he started a strafing run. As soon as he saw us, he pulled up and broke hard to starboard, and then turned to meet us head on with his 30-mm cannon. Realizing the danger, I tried to get inside his turn.

We were now down to hilltop level, and the Su-7 vanished momentarily as we rounded some high ground. He was turning incredibly tightly, and the brown earth and blue skies seemed to mingle together as we followed the low-level chase. My Mirage closed in on the Sukhoi's tail, but the G forces were too high for a clear shot. The enemy pilot was either an ace or a madman. By now the fight was down to virtually zero altitude, twisting and turning among the wadis [valleys] around Mount Hermon. The Syrian pulled some angles. He was certainly a good pilot, and I was sweating hard trying to keep up with him.

Suddenly I got my chance. Only for a moment, but I managed to fire a quick burst. The Syrian broke hard, with a small fire blossoming bright red below his wing root. Still he flew on. By now the fight was on again, as the Sukhoi frantically tried to shake me off and make a dash for home. I noticed the fire had begun to spread, and drew closer, watching the pilot struggling in the cockpit. Suddenly his aircraft blew up, engulfing my Mirage in a cloud of fire and smoke. I was temporarily blinded by the force of the explosion and felt the stick jerk in my hands. It was like hitting a brick wall in a racing car. The aircraft kicked back like a mule as I tried to roll and turn at low speed. Struggling to keep my fighter on an even keel, I managed to get clear of the fireball and flying debris. The fight was over.

MIRAGE IIIE FACT SHEET

Manufacturer: Dassault-Breguet Aviation

Type: Single-seat or twin-seat interceptor and strike aircraft

Engine: One SNECMA Atar 9C turbojet, delivering 13,200 lb. of thrust

Crew: Pilot only or pilot and systems operator

Length: 49 ft., 3½ in.

Height: 13 ft., 11½ in.

Wingspan: 27 ft.

Maximum Speed: Mach 2.2

First Flight: April 5, 1961

That's how a pilot with the Israeli Defense Force Air Force described a dogfight over the Golan Heights during the Yom Kippur War of 1973. The plane he was flying was a French-supplied Mirage III, Israel's foremost MiG killer, a title the Mirage held from 1966, when the plane first entered combat, until 1973, when it began to be replaced by the Israeli-built Kfir (cub lion) and F-15 Eagle from the United States.

The Mirage III is one of the most successful combat planes ever built. Easy to operate, easy to maintain, it has been exported by the French to every corner of the world. Over 20 air forces depend on the Mirage III as their first-line combat aircraft.

At one time, France operated approximately 450 Mirage IIIs, more than any other nation. Some versions of the plane were fitted out for air defense, others for radar attack and still others for tactical reconnaissance. And the French also had Mirage IIIEs that were meant as nuclear-strike aircraft. Each carried a 15-kiloton nuclear weapon on its centerline pylon.

By the beginning of the 1990s, well over half of France's Mirage IIIs had been withdrawn from use. Many had been replaced by the Mirage 2000 Rafale, a medium-sized, multirole fighter, which represents the next generation of French combat aircraft.

Switzerland, a nation which, like Sweden, maintains a policy of armed neutrality, has what is recognized as one of the best air forces in Europe. Switzerland's nearly 300 combat aircraft are mostly Mirage IIIs and Northrop F-5s.

This Mirage III served with France's Armée de l'Air *and carried out air defense duties.* (AeroFax)

The Royal Australian Air Force has more than 100 Mirage IIIs. Some are interceptors; others are ground-attack aircraft.

Spain operates a fleet of Mirage IIIs. In South America, the plane is favored by Brazil, Colombia, Peru, Venezuela and Argentina. Abu Dhabi, Belgium, Gabon, Libya and Saudi Arabia are other nations that have purchased the plane.

Mirage IIIs have been tested in a number of wars. Pakistan's Mirages scored eight air-to-air victories in the 1971 fighting against India. South African Mirages have been used in an air-to-ground role against neighboring states.

Argentina had about two dozen Mirage IIIs available for the Falklands War against Great Britain in 1982. But the Argentine Mirages were crippled by the hundreds of miles they had to fly from their nearest bases to the battle zone. They could remain over the Falklands for only about five minutes before having to return to the mainland for fuel. Air superiority in the Falklands belonged to Britain's AV-8B Harriers, which operated from aircraft carriers.

But it was in the Middle East—in Israel, in particular—that the Mirage III gained its greatest fame. The Israeli Defense Force Air Force began flying Mirage IIIs in 1961. Seventy-six planes were ordered that year. At the time, an uneasy truce existed between Israel and its Arab neighbors. A United Nations Emergency Force supervised the truce. In 1967, when Abdel Nasser, the president of Egypt, forced the UN peacekeepers to withdraw, tensions mounted.

What came to be known as the Six Day War broke out in June that year. Before it ended, Israel had captured Gaza and the Sinai Peninsula, and gained control of the east bank of the Suez Canal. In the six days of fighting, Israeli Mirages were credited with 48 air-to-air victories, with MiG-19s and MiG-21s the most frequent victims. Only two Mirages were lost, and both of their pilots survived.

After Israel's defeat of the Arabs in the Six Day War, France imposed an arms embargo upon Israel, refusing to sell the nation any military equipment, including additional Mirages. The Israelis responded by building, with the help of French engineers, an exact duplicate of the Mirage in their own manufacturing plants. The plane that resulted was the multimission Nesher (Eagle), which was first flown in 1969.

The years that followed the end of the Six Day War in 1967 until the outbreak of the Yom Kippur War in 1973 were anything but peaceful in Israel. The nation was frequently under attack during that period. Nevertheless, when Egypt and Syria attacked on October 6, 1973, it caught the Israeli forces by surprise. It was Yom Kippur, the Jewish Day of Atonement, the most solemn day on the Jewish calendar. Many Israeli soldiers and airmen were on leave or in a low state of readiness.

Egypt and Syria were supported by a massive airlift from the Soviet Union. The United States sent supplies and military equipment to Israel.

The Egyptian attack opened with an artillery bombardment of Israeli positions along the Suez Canal. It was followed by an attack by Egyptian ground forces, who crossed the Canal into Israel at four different points. At the same time, a strike force of over 200 Egyptian aircraft pounded Israeli military installations.

The Syrian Air Force, meanwhile, hit Israeli strongholds along the Golan plateau. Troops landing by helicopter seized Israeli observation posts on the slopes of Mount Hermon.

Israel's response was to counterattack. Israeli forces wasted no time in driving the Egyptians back and crossing the Suez Canal into Egypt. They also retook their outposts on the Golan plateau. It was over quickly. A cease-fire took effect on October 24.

The air war began within seconds after the start of hostilities and continued almost without letup until the cease-fire took effect. It pitted Mirage IIIs and Israel's Neshers against an array of Soviet-built aircraft, including Su-7s, Su-15s, MiG-21s and MiG-25s.

In the closing stages of the conflict, with Israeli forces gaining the upper hand, the Egyptians mounted a desperate effort to halt the Israeli counterattack. Big air battles became common. The Mirages and

Neshers were credited with over 300 "kills" during the brief war. Remarkably, only a handful of Israeli planes were lost.

Like many American combat aircraft, the Mirage III was developed in the years following the Korean War of 1950–53. During the war, European military experts had been impressed by the excellent flying qualities of the MiG-15. The French *Armée de l'Air* (the French Air Force) called for the development of a lightweight fighter that would be capable of climbing to an altitude of 50,000 feet in six minutes.

A team from Dassault, a company founded by Marcel Dassault in 1946, designed a small, twin-engine, delta-winged plane that was named the *Mystère Delta*. Although it was the fastest plane in France at the time, it was too small to become a practical fighter.

When redesigned, the aircraft was much more successful. It made its first flight on December 17, 1956, after having been named the Mirage I, and reached a speed of Mach 1.3 in level flight, making it one of the fastest planes in all of Europe.

More changes were proposed. A Mirage II was designed, and then a Mirage III—a tailless, delta-winged craft that won great praise from the *Armée de l'Air*. Ten prototypes were ordered.

The Mirage IIIC was the first version of the plane to reach full production. Some 95 were ordered by the *Armée de l'Air*. The aircraft gained worldwide recognition on July 22, 1962, when a production model was used by Jacqueline Auriol in becoming the first woman to fly at a speed exceeding 1,000 miles an hour. Mme. Auriol averaged 1,150 miles per hour over a closed-circuit course.

The second version of the plane to go into production was the Mirage IIIE. Earlier models of the Mirage had been mere fighters. The Mirage IIIE was a multimission combat plane. The first prototype was first flown on April 5, 1961. Over the next 25 years, the Mirage IIIE became the most successful combat aircraft ever built in Western Europe.

Other versions followed. The Mirage 5 used the airframe and engine of the Mirage IIIE, but omitted the plane's expensive avionics. This simplified version appealed to Third World countries because of its lower price.

The Mirage 50 was a more powerful version of the Mirage 5. The prototype flew for the first time in 1979.

The Mirage reached its peak of development during the mid-1980s with the Mirage IIING (for Nouvelle Génération, or New Generation). This plane offers computerized controls and the latest advances in radar and navigation systems.

Mirage III production lines were kept busy for more than 20 years. They produced some 1,400 aircraft that are flown by 21 air forces. Hundreds are in daily use. Equipment modernization programs will keep many of these aircraft active well into the 1990s. Little wonder the Mirage III has earned a place in aviation history as one of the classic jet combat aircraft.

The Mirage reached a peak of development with the production of the Mirage IIING ("NG" stands for Nouvelle Génération, New Generation) during the 1980s. (Dassault)

14   Su-27 (FLANKER)

At the Paris international air show late in the spring of 1989, the Su-27, the Soviet Union's newest long-range interceptor, with test pilot Viktor Pougachev at the controls, performed a maneuver in the daily flying sessions that dazzled the spectators. It was called "Pougachev's cobra."

Sweeping through the air on a straight right-to-left path at about 250 miles an hour, Pougachev pulled the plane's nose up until it reached a vertical position. It didn't stop there. The Soviet pilot let the nose keep swinging and within a second or two the plane was almost upside down,

Big and powerful, the Su-27 was designed for long-range interceptor missions. (Aero-Fax)

Su-27 FACT SHEET

Designer: Pavel A. Sukhoi OKB

Type: Long-range multimission fighter

Engines: Two Lyulka AL-31F turbofans, each delivering 28,000 lb. of thrust

Crew: Pilot only

Length: 69 ft.

Height: 19 ft., 8 in.

Wingspan: 47 ft., 7 in.

Loaded Weight: 44,000 lb.

Maximum Speed: Mach 2.35

First Flight: 1976

heading tail-first, briefly, in the same right-to-left direction. In reversing itself, the plane's speed had fallen to 70 or 80 miles an hour.

To recover from the stunt, Pougachev allowed the nose to swing back to its original position (a move that was said to resemble a cobra as it raises its head to strike). It took only five and a half seconds to perform the maneuver—two and a half seconds for the plane to pitch up, three seconds for it to pitch back. During that time, there was no loss of altitude.

American observers couldn't help but be impressed by Pougachev's feat, perhaps because they realized that no United States fighter was capable of performing the maneuver. Canadian pilots, however, flying F/A-18 Hornets, have performed Pougachev's cobra unintentionally during dogfights. But it is not a stunt they consider routine.

The maneuver can be very valuable in a dogfight. Suppose there's a tail-chase, one plane in close pursuit of another. The plane being chased could use Pougachev's cobra to slow down suddenly, forcing his rival to zip right by. The defender would then have an opportunity to get on his opponent's tail and perhaps end the skirmish.

One test pilot, quoted in an article in *Aviation Week and Space Technology*, applauded Pougachev's cobra. "Anyone who has ever hassled in the air knows you are mentally projecting the trajectory of the opponent all the time. If he can do something like this so he won't be where you think he will, he's got another option to use in the fight."

One of the biggest and most powerful of the Soviet fighters, the Su-27 is the latest in a long line of combat aircraft produced by the Sukhoi design bureau (named for Pavel A. Sukhoi). Others have included the Su-25 Frogfoot, a close-support and attack aircraft; the Su-24 Fencer, an all-weather attack and reconnaissance plane; and the Su-17 Fitter, a ground-attack fighter. To the Soviet air forces, the Sukhoi design bureau is second in importance only to the Mikoyan/Gurevich OKB, the maker of MiGs.

One reason the Su-27 is so big is because its size was dictated, at least in part, by the need to have a large radar antenna. The radar dish inside the plane demanded a fuselage four feet in diameter. The Su-27 is 69 feet in length, which is longer by several feet than the F-15, the biggest American fighter. The Su-27 is, in fact, larger in all its dimensions than the F-15, a plane that is itself sometimes jokingly referred to as a "flying tennis court."

The Su-27 was designed for long, overwater interception or patrol missions. Yet it lacks the capability to be refueled while in the air. This is not a terribly serious failing, however, for the aircraft can carry up to 10 tons of fuel, which translates into a maximum range of 2,580 miles. That's two or three times the range of most American fighters.

Its two Lyulka turbofans enable the Su-27 to exceed twice the speed of sound.
(AeroFax)

There are actually two versions of the Su-27. One is the single-seat model that performed Pougachev's cobra at the Paris air show. This version serves not only as a trainer but also as a long-range interceptor or patrol aircraft. For extended training flights, a two-seat version is used. Both seats are occupied by pilots, one of whom relieves the other.

Like other Soviet fighters, the twin-engine Su-27 was designed for use on rough, unpaved airstrips. It has protective screens over the air inlets of its engines to prevent the pickup of foreign objects. It also has a heavy-duty landing gear. This is useful in permitting the plane to be operated by inexperienced pilots, who are frequently guilty of making hard landings.

When the Su-27 was first planned, the F-14 Tomcat and the F-15 Eagle were already tried and proven as combat aircraft. The Soviet plane was thus able to draw upon the technology and design that went into both of the American fighters. For example, the Su-27 is the first Soviet fighter to be equipped with "fire and forget" air-to-air missiles. Once the Su-27's radar has locked-in on a hostile target, there's no need for the pilot to keep flying toward the target. He can turn away and go after other targets. The missiles he's fired will seek out the original target. American fighters have had this capability since the mid-1980s.

The cobra maneuver performed by the Su-27 subjects the plane to loads of three and a half to four Gs. This occurs during the early stages, when the plane's speed plummets from 250 miles an hour to 70 to 80 miles an hour in just two and a half seconds.

Mikhail Simonov, head of the Sukhoi design bureau, once explained that Pougachev's cobra was originally "a test-program maneuver to help determine the upper-limit angle of attack for the flight-control system."

Said Simonov: "When it was decided to sent the Su-27 to Paris, we wanted something with show quality to impress people. The pilots who were planning the flight demonstration recalled the maneuver and incorporated it into the sequence."

It was a wise decision. The Su-27 is an outstanding plane. It's very fast—faster than the F-16 or F/A-18. It has tremendous range and can carry a heavy missile load. But it's probably best known around the world for its ability to perform Pougachev's cobra.

15   F-117 STEALTH

Employing low-observable technology, the F-117 Stealth is designed to penetrate "dense threat" environments and attack "high-value" targets. (U.S. Air Force)

Hump-backed, wedge-nosed, with twin rudders that sweep back sharply to form a V tail, Lockheed's F-117 doesn't look like what we're used to fighter planes looking like. That's because it's no ordinary aircraft. Called the Black Jet by its pilots, it's the first fighter—the first combat plane of any time—to employ low-observable technology. That means it presents some tricky problems to enemy radar transmitters.

The F-117 is a single-seat, twin-engine fighter. But it is not a fighter in the classic sense of being designed to mix it up in combat with enemy

F-117 FACT SHEET

Manufacturer: Lockheed Aeronautical System Company

Type: Low-observable attack aircraft

Engines: Two General Electric F404 engines, each delivering 12,000 lb. of thrust

Crew: Pilot only

Length: 65 ft., 11 in.

Height: 12 ft., 5 in.

Wingspan: 38 ft., 5 in.

Loaded Weight: 52,500 lb.

Maximum Speed: Mach 1+

First Flight: 1981

fighter planes. The F-117 is a medium-altitude, air-to-surface strike fighter. Its role is more like that of the F-111 than the F-16.

The F-117 was first used in combat during the American invasion of Panama late in 1989. The following year, when President George Bush called for a major deployment of United States military forces in Saudi Arabia, in answer to Iraq's invasion of Kuwait, 22 F-117s (more than one-third of the total force) were hurriedly dispatched to the Middle East, to be stationed within striking distance of Iraqi military targets.

In mid-January, when the United States went to war against Iraq, the F-117 established itself as the star of the air combat campaign. It didn't happen overnight, however.

In the early days of the conflict, F-15s, F-16s and F/A-18s were used in an effort to destroy Iraqi bridges. After more than 100 missions, the bridges remained standing.

American military planners then turned to F-117s (and F-111s) armed with 500-pound laser-guided bombs. Seven bridges were destroyed the first night.

During the war, which lasted 43 days, more than 1,200 combat aircraft from 11 countries flew for the allied cause. F-117s represented only 2% to 3% of that number. Yet the plane struck 43% of the Iraqi targets that were hit, said the Air Force.

That kind of success had enormous impact on American military leaders. "We've always looked at warfare as being speed, mass, and surprise," said Brig. Gen. Buster C. Glosson, a principal architect of the air campaign against Iraq. "I believe we changed that forever to speed, precision, and surprise."

The idea for a "stealth" combat plane goes back many years, to a time when problems of radar detection were becoming critical—that is, to that time when weapons controlled by radar began knocking aircraft out of the sky with some regularity. During the war in Vietnam, Soviet-supplied SAMs—surface-to-air missiles—enabled the North Vietnamese to take a heavy toll of American tactical aircraft and bombers. In 1972 alone, during the last major aerial campaign of the war, SAMs claimed 16 of the huge B-52 bombers. The following year, 1973, during the Yom Kippur War, Egyptian SAMs tormented the Israeli Air Force.

While electronic countermeasures could sometimes thwart surface-to-air missiles, something more effective was needed—a defense system that would enable a plane to escape radar detection. "Stealth" was the term used to describe the project.

The Lockheed Corporation was named prime contractor for the Stealth fighter. The first test flights of demonstration versions of the new plane took place during the late 1970s at a super-secret airfield north of Las Vegas called "the ranch." The airfield was part of an enormous complex of restricted airfields and ranges known as Dreamland (where the Air Force also reportedly flew Soviet MiGs).

Lockheed was said to have produced three prototypes, two of which crashed. The accidents were blamed on the wish to get the aircraft operational as soon as possible, as well as the perils always associated with test-flying, rather than any failing of the Stealth technology itself.

In 1980s, *Armed Forces Journal* revealed that the United States had been flying a "virtually invisible" aircraft for years. Shortly after the article appeared, Harold Brown, Secretary of Defense under President Jimmy Carter, confirmed that the Air Force had, in fact, been test-flying an airplane that was difficult for radar to detect.

Brown added to the exaggerated claims that were being made on behalf of the aircraft by saying, "It cannot be successfully intercepted with existing air-defense systems." Brown also boasted that the development "alters the military balance in favor of the United States."

The Carter administration was criticized for going public with the Stealth. The President, who was seeking reelection that year, was said to have been motivated by political reasons. Although political considerations were surely involved, the foremost reason for the disclosure was that the project was simply getting too big to hide in the budget. In 1981 alone, the United States was said to have spent about a billion dollars on Stealth research.

Despite the revelations, official spokesmen for both the Air Force and Lockheed continued to deny the Stealth fighter existed. To any questions, they replied, "We have no knowledge of such a project."

It was later learned that Lockheed's Advanced Development Project was awarded a contract in 1978 to produce the new plane. The Stealth's first flight took place in 1981.

The project was officially known as COSIR, from Covert Survivable In-weather Reconnaissance Strike. For a time, the plane was designated the F-19A and called the Aurora. The names Specter and Gray Ghost were also applied to the aircraft—and even the name Harvey, for the invisible rabbit in the movie of the same name that starred Jimmy Stewart.

Despite the fact that the public knew about the plane, the project continued to be surrounded by secrecy and rumor. Artists' impressions of what the Stealth looked like appeared regularly in newspapers and magazines. There were even model kits offered for sale (all of which were completely wrong in their conception of the plane's appearance).

Fifty-nine F-117s were ordered by the Air Force. All were in operation by the end of 1990. (Lockheed Aeronautical Systems; Eric Schulzinger)

The Stealth fighter's existence was officially acknowledged by the Air Force in 1988, five years after it had entered operational service. At that time, the Air Force began operating the plane in the daylight as well as at night.

Finally, on April 21, 1990, at Nellis Air Force Base near Las Vegas, Nevada, the F-117 was introduced to the public. By the end of 1990, 59 F-117s were in operation. Their total cost was put at $6½ billion—a figure that included $2 billion in development costs, according to the Department of Defense.

Pilots who fly the F-117 are volunteers who have experience in flying strike fighters, particularly the F-111. Each must have a minimum of 1,000 hours of flight time. During their two-year tour of duty with the F-117, each pilot flies the aircraft from 15 to 20 hours a week.

Each of the F-117's twin General Electric F404 engines produces 12,000 pounds of thrust, propelling the aircraft at a speed of just beyond Mach 1. The plane has a range of about 800 miles, nearly twice that of the F/A-18.

When America was seeking reprisal against Libya in 1986 for assorted acts of violence and an air strike was decided upon, the F-117 was, for a time, given consideration as the plane to carry out the mission. The plan was to deploy Stealth fighters at a base in Sicily. Sending the plane to

An F-117 Stealth gets refueled from a KC-10A Extender. (Lockheed Aeronautical Systems; Eric Schulzinger)

Libya and back would have been within the F-117's 800-mile operating range. But the mission was eventually handed to the F-111s based in England.

Of course, the F-117's range can be boosted through in-flight refueling. The plane can also be shuttled long distances by folding or removing its wings and packing it aboard a C-15 Galaxy transport plane.

The F-117 is not an aircraft that is invisible to radar. That idea is laughable. But it was designed so that its chances of being detected by radar are very much reduced. The Stealth is what is called a "low-observable" aircraft.

The plane's designers relied on the concept of "faceting" to give the F-117 as small a radar signature as possible. The skin panels of the plane's arrow-shaped airframe are divided into small, irregular, flat surfaces. These panels reflect the radar signals from enemy aircraft, or hostile ground radars, at many different angles. This produces confusion on enemy radar screens.

The F-117's missiles and bombs, its auxiliary fuel tanks and other external stores are carried inside the plane where they can't serve as targets for enemy radar. (Lockheed Aeronautical Systems; Eric Schulzinger)

So the F-117 doesn't really evade radar, as some sources once said it could. Instead, it sends back distorted radar signals.

There are no Sparrows, Sidewinders or other missiles suspended from the wing of the F-117. There are no fuel cells or external stores of any kind hanging there. These would be easy targets for radar. Anything the Stealth carries is concealed inside the plane's airframe.

The spinning turbine blades of the standard jet engine are another of radar's favorite sights. So the air intake of the F-117's engine has been mounted above the wing and rear fuselage, and thus is shielded from ground radar.

Heat-seeking air-to-air missiles normally target on the hot exhaust gases emitted by jet engines. Designers of the F-117 managed to overcome this hazard. The plane's twin engines, which are the same as those in the F/A-18, have had their afterburners replaced with huge exhaust pipes. In these, the hot exhaust gases are mixed with masses of cold air. This produces a cool and almost undetectable exhaust output.

The stealth-like qualities of the F-117 are also apparent in the aircraft's carbon-fiber skin. This tends to absorb radar signals, rather than bounce them back.

The Stealth has been designed to penetrate what the Air Force calls "dense threat environments" and attack "high-value targets" with pinpoint accuracy. What is a high-value target? An enemy command post, surface-to-air missile site, hardened aircraft shelter, and the like.

Most sources agree that the AGM-65 Maverick family of missiles would be the most likely ordnance for the F-117 to carry. The Maverick is a "launch-and-leave," television-guided, air-to-surface missile. It enables the pilot, once he has sent the missile on its way, to exit the target area. He doesn't have to remain locked on the target to provide a missile path.

There are several different versions of the Maverick. The AGM-65B offers "scene magnification." This enables the pilot to identify and target on smaller and more distant objects.

For nighttime missions, there's the AGM-65D, which boasts IIR (imagery infrared seeker), and the AGM-65G, which also uses IIR but has a 298-pound fragmentation warhead.

Critics of the F-117 claim that it is a relatively unstable aircraft, one that requires sophisticated on-board computers to constantly make flight corrections. And when the computers don't function properly, the plane "does its own thing." It can "get away" from the pilot, who then has to take over manually. For that reason, some pilots are said to have dubbed the F-117 the "wobbly goblin."

But others of those who have flown the plane say that it is highly maneuverable, with good handling characteristics. "The F-117's image as an unstable aircraft is not correct," according to Ted Morganfeld, a Lockheed test pilot. "It does not merit the 'wobbly goblin' nickname."

The F-117's control system is the same as that used on the F-16. Its cockpit displays are from the F/A-18, while the control stick is Lockheed's design.

According to Morganfeld, visibility from the cockpit is satisfactory, despite the three-piece, triangular-shaped windshield. Visibility to the front and side are better than to the rear, where the view is blocked somewhat by the canopy.

Once inside the cockpit, the pilot does not have to take any particular "low-observable" precautions, according to *Aviation Week and Space Technology* magazine. He wears a standard flight suit and operates as would the pilot of any other combat aircraft.

In its first combat mission, the F-117 did nothing to quiet those who have criticized the plane. The mission took place during America's invasion of Panama late in 1989. Shortly after the invasion began, Secretary of Defense Richard Cheney announced that each of two F-111s and F-117s had delivered a 2,000-pound bomb with "pinpoint accuracy." The bombs, dropped close to a military barracks, were supposed to stun Panamanian soldiers without killing them.

But early the following year, after a reporter from the *New York Times* showed pictures of the bombed site to Pentagon officials, Secretary Cheney learned that the bombs had missed their targets. In the attack, one of the bombs, which was supposed to have fallen about 100 yards from the barracks for the seventh company of Panamanian forces, fell instead almost 300 yards from the structure. The other bomb was also way off target. While the misses made little difference in the overall success of the invasion, they were an embarrassment for Air Force officials who had praised the F-117 for its precision.

But in the Persian Gulf in 1991, the F-117 redeemed itself. It was, for example, the only plane flown inside the city of Baghdad, where precision bombing was vital. "To do the things that we did in Baghdad in the old days would have taken large numbers of bombs with a lot of damage to surrounding areas," said Lieut. Gen. Charles A. Horner, the commander of allied air forces in the Gulf. "These guys went out there night after night and took out individual buildings."

At war's end, General Horner, in an interview with the *New York Times*, declared that "...the war had established that radar-evading "stealth" technology and the pinpoint accuracy of precision-guided bombs were changing the nature of air warfare." You can't expect any higher praise than that.

AIRCRAFT DESIGNATION SYSTEM

Planes of the United States Air Force, Navy and Marine Corps are classified by a coded system of letters and numbers. The letters indicate the plane's mission; the numbers refer to the plane's model.

Here are the various mission symbols.

SYMBOL	MISSION
A	Attack
B	Bomber
C	Cargo/transport
E	Electronics
F	Fighter
K	Tanker
L	Liason
O	Observation
P	Patrol
Q	Targeting and drone
R	Reconnaissance
S	Search and rescue
T	Trainer
U	Utility
X	Research

As an example, planes designated F-4 or F-14 are fighters. The "4" and "14" indicate the particular model.

Letters that follow the model number indicate a modification, such as F-4C or F-14D.

Two other symbols are used to indicate aircraft type. They are:

H	Helicopter
V	VTOL (vertical takeoff and landing) or STOL (short takeoff and landing).

An additional letter is sometimes used before the other letters or numbers. This prefix indicates that the aircraft has a special status.

LETTER	STATUS
G	Permanently grounded
J	Special test, temporary
N	Special test, permanent
X	Experimental
Y	Prototype
Z	In planning or development

GLOSSARY

afterburner A device on the engine of a jet airplane that provides for extra thrust by burning additional fuel in the hot exhaust gases.

angle of attack The angle of a plane's wing relative to the forward flight of the aircraft.

avionics Aeronautical electronics.

bandit Bad guy in a dogfight.

bingo Minimum fuel required for a safe and comfortable return to one's base.

bogey Unidentified and potentially hostile aircraft.

bolter A carrier landing attempt in which the plane's hook fails to engage an arresting cable, causing the plane to make another attempt.

burner Short for afterburner (see afterburner).

combat radius The maximum operational capability of an aircraft, measured from its base to the area where it carries out its mission.

dogfight A violent aerial battle between two fighter planes at close quarters.

flak Antiaircraft fire.

flap The moving control surface on the trailing edge of an aircraft wing.

flare The nose-up landing attitude of land-based fighters. Carrier jets forego flare in favor of slam-down landings.

fly-by-wire Computer-controlled operation of aircraft control surfaces, such as the ailerons and elevators. The F-16, F/A-18 and MiG-31 are among those aircraft that use fly-by-wire controls.

foreplane A winglike structure positioned on the fuselage just forward and slightly higher than the main wing.

G A unit of force equal to the gravity exerted on a body at rest. At one G, a 200-pound man weights 200 pounds; at four Gs, he weighs 800 pounds. In airplanes, G forces develop in rapid turns, climbs and dives.

G-suit Nylon trousers that wrap around the legs and belly, and fill automatically with air in high-G maneuvers.

intercept To detect and destroy enemy aircraft.

interdict To cut or destroy enemy lines of communication and supply.

Mach A number used to describe the speed of planes flying near or above the speed of sound. At Mach 1, a plane is traveling at the speed of sound. (At 40,000 feet, sound normally travels at 660 miles an hour.) At Mach 2, a plane is traveling at twice the speed of sound (about 1,320 miles an hour). The term is named after Ernest Mach, an Austrian physicist who died in 1916.

ordnance Military weapons, especially heavy guns and ammunition.

pass The point at which a pair of fighters, closing head-on, rush past one another.

pit The rear-seat position of a two-seat aircraft, such as the F-14.

pole Slang for the control stick.

prototype The original model of an aircraft.

pylon A curved or angular piece of metal that is used to hold or suspend various types of bombs, missiles or fuel pods from an aircraft's wings or fuselage.

range The maximum distance an airplane can travel.

reconnaissance An aerial exploration of an area to gather military information.

speed jeans Slang for G suit.

squadron A group of four or more aircraft of the same type.

subsonic Having a speed less than the speed of sound.

supersonic Having a speed greater than the speed of sound.

thrust The forward force created in a jet engine as a reaction to the rearward ejection of fuel gases at high velocities.

trap Arrested aircraft-carrier landing.

vector The direction followed by an airplane.

wingman Pilot of the second plane in a two-aircraft formation.

ABBREVIATIONS AND ACRONYMS

AAA Antiaircraft artillery

AB Air base

ADC Air Defense Command

AFCS Automatic flight control system

AGM Air-to-ground missile

AIM Air intercept missile

AMRAAM Advanced medium-range air-to-air missile

AMSA Advanced manned strategic aircraft

ANG Air National Guard

ARM Anti-radiation missile; an air-to-surface missile designed to home in on the radiation emitted by radar transmitters

ASM Air-to-surface missile

ASRAAM Advanced short-range air-to-air missile

ASW Anti-submarine warfare

ATA Air tactical aircraft

ATC Air Training Command

ATF Advanced tactical fighter

AWACS Airborne warning and control system

BIT Built-in test (equipment); common to most electronic and avionic systems

BVR Beyond visual range

CAP Combat air patrol

CAS Close air support

CBU Cluster bomb unit

CO Commanding officer

CRT Cathode ray tube; video display terminal

ECM Electronic countermeasures; special equipment to overcome or lessen the effectiveness of enemy guidance and fire-control systems

ELINT Electronic intelligence

EW Electronic warfare

EWO Electronic warfare officer

FMC Fully mission capable

GSE Ground support equipment

HARM High-speed anti-radiation missile

HAWK Homing all the way killer; standard U.S. medium-range surface-to-air missile system

HOTAS Hands on throttle and stick; the cockpit design followed by the U.S. Air Force

HUD Head-up display; a video screen mounted above the forward instrument panel that displays computer-generated navigation and weapons-system information

IFF Identification, friend or foe; electronic devices designed to determine which unidentified aircraft are friendly and which are enemies

IIR Imaging infrared (seeker)

INS Internal navigation system

IR Infrared

LRU Line replaceable unit

MAC Military Airlift Command

MR Mission ready

NASA National Aeronautics and Space Administration

NATO North Atlantic Treaty Organization

PGM Precision-guided munitions; also called "smart bombs"

RAF Royal Air Force; the air arm of the United Kingdom

RAG Replacement air group

RCAF Royal Canadian Air Force

RIO Radio intercept officer

RPV Remotely piloted vehicle

SAC Strategic Air Command

SAM   Surface-to-air missile

STOL   Short takeoff and landing

TAC   Tactical Air Command

TACAN   Tactical air navigation; a navigational system that locates an aircraft relative to an electronic beacon

TFS   Tactical fighter squadron

TFTS   Tactical fighter training squadron

TFTW   Tactical fighter training wing

TFW   Tactical fighter wing

USAF   United States Air Force

USAFE   United States Air Forces in Europe

VID   Visual identification

VIFF   Vectoring in forward flight

V/STOL   Vertical/short takeoff and landing

VTOL   Vertical takeoff and landing

WSO   Weapons systems operator

INDEX

BIOGRAPHY

George Sullivan, author of a good-sized shelf of books for young readers, often writes about military aviation. His titles include *The Thunderbirds*, a profile of the Air Force's famed demonstration squadron, and *Famous Air Force Bombers*.

In gathering information for his books, Mr. Sullivan often visits aircraft carriers and air bases, interviewing pilots and aircraft support personnel. He is a member of the Tailhook Association, an organization of pilots, air crew members and others who have made carrier-arrested landings. A former Navy journalist, Mr. Sullivan lives in New York City.